# CHILE

## A PRIMARY SOURCE CULTURAL GUIDE

Jason Porterfield
and
Corona Brezina

The Rosen Publishing Group's
PowerPlus Books™
New York

Published in 2004 by The Rosen Publishing Group, Inc.
29 East 21st Street, New York, NY 10010

**Library of Congress Cataloging-in-Publication Data**

Porterfield, Jason.
Chile: a primary source cultural guide / by Jason Porterfield and Corona Brezina.— 1st ed.
  p. cm. — (Primary sources of world cultures)
Summary: An overview of the history and culture of Chile and its people including the geography, myths, arts, daily life, education, industry, and government, with illustrations from primary source documents.     52905   Chile : a primary source cultural guide
Includes bibliographical references and index.
ISBN 0-8239-3837-9 (library binding)
1. Chile—Juvenile literature. [1. Chile.] I. Brezina, Corona. II. Title. III. Series.
F3058.5.P67 2003
983—dc21
                                                                                    2002156675

*Manufactured in the United States of America*

**Cover images:** Historic pageant at elementary school in Valparaiso (right), Plaza de la Constitucion in Santiago (center), Rongorongo tablets on Easter Island (background).

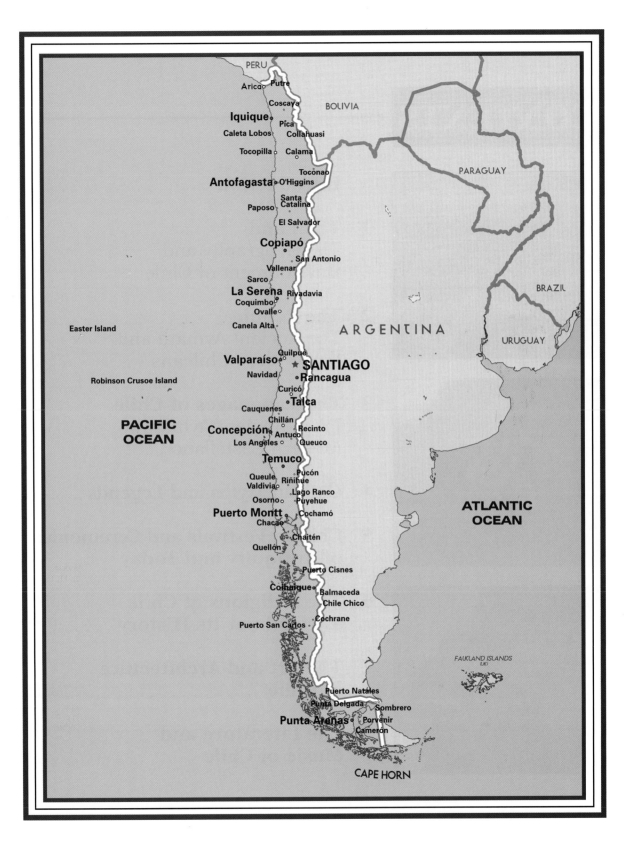

# CONTENTS

# INTRODUCTION

**C**hile hugs the western coast of South America, with the sweeping Pacific coastline to the west and the rugged Andes mountains to the east. In the arid northern regions, abandoned mining towns dot the Atacama Desert, the driest spot in the world. Far to the south, researchers conduct experiments within another type of desert, Chile's Antarctic territory. In between these inhospitable extremes, most of the Chilean population lives in the temperate and fertile Central Valley.

More than a dozen millennia ago, humans first settled the land now known as Chile. In the sixteenth century, the Spaniards arrived and began to conquer the descendants of these original settlers.

Some 250 years later, most of the population consisted of mestizos, the mixed-blood descendants of Spanish colonists and indigenous peoples. They rebelled against Spain, and the world recognized an independent Republic of Chile in 1818.

Chile, in one of the more isolated corners of the earth, reaches out to the world with its exports. Every day, millions of people worldwide use products containing Chilean copper,

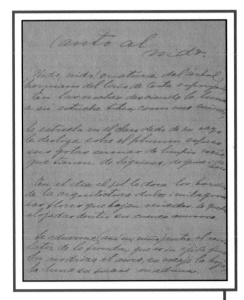

The Atacama Desert *(left)* is composed of salt basins, sand, and lava flows, and it stretches from the Pacific Ocean to the Andes. Even though this area is on the ocean, the Atacama receives little to no rainfall because the ocean currents keep clouds off the coastline. Atacama is so desolate that it is sometimes described as moonlike, and in fact, it has been the test site for prototypes of lunar rovers. A poem titled "Canto al nido" *(above)* was written by Chilean writer Gabriela Mistral. She won the Nobel Prize for literature in 1945. In 1981, to honor her, the country introduced a 500-peso note, the highest denomination in Chile, with a portrait of Mistral. Mistral is the first famous woman to be pictured on currency in Chile.

drink Chilean wines, and purchase high-quality Chilean fruit in supermarkets. But Chile's most significant contributions to the world are far less tangible. For instance, the Nobel Prize–winning poets Gabriela Mistral (1889–1957) and Pablo Neruda (1904–1973) wrote timeless and inspiring poetry. But Chile also produced the dictator Augusto Pinochet (b. 1915), who led the government from 1974 to 1990. For most of its existence, Chile has enjoyed relative stability as a democratic nation. Because of Pinochet, however, outsiders will long associate the country's name with repression and violence committed by a dictatorial government.

Today, many of Chile's people still grapple with Pinochet's legacy, while others have put his regime behind them. Northern herders look after llamas and alpacas as they have since before Europeans arrived in the region. Urban commuters leave their high-rise apartments for jobs in the bustling business districts. Social reformers are pleased with some of the new programs being enacted, while businesspeople cheer the country's healthy economic situation. Chile's high rate of poverty is gradually lowering. The country is on a path of economic and social progress, yet the indigenous Mapuche people still manage to observe their vibrant native culture. Parents still dote on their children, and people value time spent with extended family members. Chilean children anticipate a bright future.

There are no major river systems in Chile. Instead, there are short rivers that begin in the Andes and flow west to the Pacific Ocean. These rivers are unnavigable because of rapids and cascades; however, they are important as a renewable energy source. Hydroelectric power stations, such as this one located on the Rapel River, produce about half of Chile's electricity. The energy demand in Chile has increased rapidly, averaging about 7 percent annually since 1992. This significant growth has come from energy demands by the mining industry and growing populations in urban areas.

# THE LAND

## The Geography and Environment of Chile

**A**n old Chilean tale says that after God created the world, he had a few leftover fragments. Scattering them along the coast of South America, he created Chile, a country of deserts and glaciers, mountains and fertile plains. Today the people of Chile depend heavily on the natural resources of the land. Many Chileans work in agriculture, forestry, and mining.

Nicknamed "the thin country," Chile is longer than the distance between New York and San Francisco. Its land area is 292,133 square miles (756,621 square kilometers), almost twice the size of California. Chile extends for 2,647 miles (4,270 km), but has an average width of only 110 miles (177 km). People compare its shape to a string bean. It is the fourth largest country in South America, bordered by Peru to the north and Bolivia and Argentina to the east.

Natural barriers have influenced Chile's development more than political boundaries. Three geographical features make up the country's narrow width. The Andes mountain range forms a wall to the east. West of the Andes lie Chile's central flatlands. These exist as a desert plateau in the north and turn into the fertile Central Valley farther south. To the west run long, coastal cordilleras, a semimountainous range with an average height of 3,280 feet (1,000 meters). In the far

The Bío-Bío (*left*), which winds through lava rock canyons and volcanoes, is where the indigenous Mapuche held off the Spanish conquistadors. This separation remains; today, the area north of the river is Spanish dominated, while the Mapuche predominate in the south. More than one million people of all ethnicities use the river's resources for drinking, irrigation, recreation, and fisheries. Panquehue (*above*), in the Aconcagua Valley, is home to the Viña Errazuriz vineyard. Founded in 1870, it has become the world's largest privately owned vineyard and is currently the fifth largest exporter of wines from Chile.

Reserva Nacional las Chinchillas (Chinchilla National Reservation), in the Choapa Valley, is the only reservation in the world that protects the chinchilla, an endangered rodent. Approximately 6,000 chinchillas inhabit this land. The endangered small wildcat also lives on the reservation along with raptors such as owls, hawks, and eagles and small birds like quail and loica. The *Echinopsis chiloensis*, a cactus that can reach a height of up to twenty-five feet, is indigenous to Chile.

south, the central flatlands and the coastal cordilleras break up into an archipelago, a series of tiny islands. The vast Pacific Ocean lies to Chile's west.

The country sits on two major tectonic plates—interlocking pieces of the earth's crust that are prone to movement. The gradual collision of these huge masses—the Nazca Plate and the South American Plate—thousands of years ago, resulted in the formation of the Andes. They continue to move, causing frequent seismic disturbances.

Chileans are accustomed to minor ground tremors. However, earthquakes have destroyed areas of Chile throughout its history. In 1939, a quake killed 28,000 people and left tens of thousands homeless. A massive earthquake in 1960 triggered tidal waves and a series of volcanic eruptions, killing 2,000 people and devastating the city of Valdivia.

Chile also lies in the Ring of Fire, an area of seismic and volcanic activity at the rim of the Pacific Ocean. Out of 2,085 volcanoes in Chile, more than 50 are active or semiactive. In the northern mountains, Ojos del Salado is the world's highest active volcano. At 22,614 feet (6,893 m), it is also Chile's highest peak.

# Regions

Chile's northernmost region, El Norte Grande, "the great north," contains a region of the Atacama Desert, the driest spot in the world. Since people began recording rainfall, some parts of the desert have never received rain. Under the rocks and sand lie mineral deposits, including a fifth of the world's copper reserves and nitrates that fueled Chile's economy before World War I (1914–1918). The huge mine at Chuquicamata is the world's single largest source of copper.

El Norte Grande is famous for geoglyphs left by prehistoric peoples who created geometric designs and huge depictions of humans and animals on mountains and dunes. Some are nearly 400 feet (122 m) wide. One of the more unusual natural sights is the Valle de la Luna, or Valley of the Moon. The harsh elements shaped eerie sculptures in this lifeless expanse of gypsum, clay, and salt. In the foothills or on the altiplano of the Andes, the Aymara peoples raise llamas and alpacas. Also in the lower mountains are the spectacular El Tatio geysers. At approximately 14,110 feet (4,300 m), they are the highest in the world. To the south, El Norte Chico, or "little north," is a semiarid region that allows some irrigated farming. It relies heavily on tourism and is known for growing grapes for *pisco*, a Chilean brandy.

The remains of an abandoned office waste away on the nitrate-rich Atacama Desert. An important part of Chile's economy, nitrates are used to produce gunpowder and construction materials and to conduct electricity. Unfortunately, nitrate mining has created soil erosion and water pollution. It has killed nearby plants and animals, and has caused health problems for miners. Attempting to reverse the damage, the government of Chile has passed legislation to regulate the industry and protect the environment.

Ninety percent of the population lives in Chile's temperate and fertile Central Valley. More than one-third of all Chileans inhabit Gran Santiago, which includes the capital and its surrounding suburbs. With about 5.5 million people, it is the fifth largest city in South America, the only one in Chile with a population of more than 500,000 residents.

Other major cities include Concepción, Viña del Mar, and Valparaíso, Chile's largest port. The Mediterranean climate, along with ample rainfall and sun, make the Central Valley ideal for agriculture. The soil is particularly fertile here because of the Aconcagua and Bío-Bío Rivers. Farmers grow wheat, potatoes, fruit, vegetables, and other crops. Ranchers raise cattle, horses, and sheep.

The central region below the Bío-Bío River is sometimes called the Frontier. Here, the fierce Mapuche Indians held out against European settlers until the mid-nineteenth century. Today, the Mapuche live on reservations in Los Lagos, the Lake District, a hilly forested region dotted with volcanoes. It is named for its beautiful looking-glass lakes, including Lago Llanquihue, the fourth largest in South America. The important cities of this region are Valdivia, influenced by an influx of German settlers, and the busy port city of Puerto Montt. Much of the population lives on small farms.

South of Puerto Montt, the country breaks up into an archipelago. The fragmentation begins at the large island of Chiloé. Hundreds of small islands extend down the coastline to the tip of South America. The southern third of the country may be even more inhospitable than the dry northern region. It has a population density of only one or two people per square mile. Inlets and fjords wind among islands, crooked peninsulas, mountains, and glaciers.

When explorers first visited the tip of South America, they met natives wearing thick boots. They dubbed the land Patagonia, meaning "big feet"! Chile and Argentina share ownership of Patagonia and Tierra del Fuego, an island at the tip of South America. A large part of Chilean Patagonia has been designated the Torres del Paine National Park. Its name refers to the three "needles" of rock towering over the land. Between the mainland and Tierra del Fuego runs the Strait of Magellan, which is named for the Portuguese explorer Ferdinand Magellan, the first European man known to have sailed around the tip of South America. Small islands known as Cape Horn lie south of Tierra del Fuego.

Torres del Paine National Park, called the park at the end of the world, has incredible peaks and mountains that formed 12 million years ago. On the southern tip of Chile and encompassing 598,000 acres, the park has hiking paths that reveal distinct ecosystems, each one containing landscapes, plants, and wildlife found nowhere else in the world.

Chile owns several Pacific islands. Easter Island is the most famous. Indigenous people call it Rapa Nui. People have long been intrigued by the mysteries of its gigantic, brooding moai statues. It is the most isolated island in the world, being some 1,180 miles (1,900 km) away from any other island and 2,300 miles (3,700 km) from Chile. Three volcanoes, now dormant, created the island, which is covered by grassy hills and is riddled with caves.

Chile's lesser-known possessions include the three islands of the Juan Fernández Archipelago, 416 miles (670 km) from the Chilean mainland. Chile also claims a territory in Antarctica, where it operates five scientific bases. The Chilean Antarctic Territory overlaps with British and Argentine claims. The Antarctic Treaty of 1959 prevents any country from claiming exclusive control over any Antarctic land.

## Climate and Environment

Chile's climate becomes colder and wetter from north to south, considering the country's great length. The Humboldt current, running along the coastline, keeps air and water cool even in the northern desert region. The mountains to the east also help ease temperature extremes. The average temperature of the northern desert is 69°F (20°C) in midsummer, and the extreme south rarely falls far below the average temperature of 32°F (0°C), even in winter. Seasons are reversed from those in the Northern Hemisphere. In Chile, winter lasts from May to July.

While the north is arid, there is ample precipitation for crops in the Central Valley. The south receives more rain than any other place in the world outside of rain forests, up to 216 inches

Five million people live in Santiago, the capital and largest city in Chile. Within view of the Andes mountains, Santiago is one of the only cities in the world where people have easy access to both beaches and ski slopes.

(538 cm) annually. Chiloé sees only 60 days of sun per year and may experience 150 stormy days. Severe, unpredictable weather sweeps across the desolate far south.

Recently, Chile has begun to examine some of its environmental problems. Santiago is usually enveloped in a haze of air pollution from vehicles and factories. Industry, especially copper mining in the north, creates hazardous emissions. Toxic runoff drains into water supplies and destroys the habitats of native plants and animals. Agricultural firms use huge amounts of herbicides and pesticides on their crops.

Many rivers run east from the Andes, providing prime cropland on banks and river valleys. This rushing mountain water has great potential for hydroelectric energy. When the government announced plans to dam the Bío-Bío, the idea was met with controversy because it could harm the environment as well as the livelihoods of the Mapuche, people who depend on the land around the river.

## Plants and Animals

Chile contains less biodiversity than its neighbors, but there is no lack of wildlife. A variety of plants and animals have adapted to Chile's many

## The Camelid Family

Long before the Spanish arrived, Chile's indigenous people herded and hunted llamas, alpacas, guanacos, and vicuñas. These woolly deer-like creatures, related to camels, are well adapted to the rugged Chilean landscape. The smallest of the camelids are the endangered vicuñas. Many live in areas that are now national parks. Humans treasure their fine golden wool, once used for the garments of Incan rulers. The larger guanacos roam throughout the countryside and can sometimes be seen swimming between coastal islands. Tamed llamas, used as pack animals, have a reputation for foul tempers. One of the camelids' few defenses against predators is spitting at them. Alpacas, which are slightly smaller than llamas and guanacos, live almost wild in herds tended by the Aymara peoples. Once a year, the Aymara round up the surefooted creatures to villages on the plains and shear the alpacas' thick wool.

biomes, from the desert to forests, plains to mountains. The composition of a forest depends on its geographic region. Different areas include coniferous and deciduous woodlands. Chile has thirty national parks and many other nature preserves, sanctuaries, and monuments. The government permits some commercial use of resources on national land.

Two of Chile's most distinctive trees are the coniferous *Araucaria araucana*, or monkey puzzle tree, and the alerce tree, related to the cypress. These can live for thousands of years, but their numbers have been diminished by logging. Cacti thrive in the northern desert. The copihue, the national flower, grows in the Lake District.

Some of Chile's animal life includes pumas, Andean wolves, the large Chilean bullfrog, endangered chilote foxes, two kinds of poisonous spiders, the ostrichlike ñandú, wild mountain cats, rodents (such as the rabbitlike viscachas), and the Andean condor, Chile's national bird. Lizards and exotic insects have adapted to Chile's varying climates. Seabirds and mammals live on the coast, including penguins, pelicans, petrels, otters, and seals.

Many of Chile's native species have been decimated by hunting and loss of habitat. Flamingos, who live in the altiplano wetlands have dwindled to about seven thousand. The llaca is the only marsupial species surviving in the southern Andes. Some of the last wild chinchillas, prized for their fur, inhabit the high altiplano. Chile is also home to the endangered huemul, a large deer featured on the Chilean coat of arms, and the endangered pudú, the world's smallest deer.

The *Araucaria araucana*, or monkey puzzle tree *(left)*, indigenous to Chile and Argentina, is about sixty million years old. The name was coined by an Englishman in the 1800s who thought the tree would be a puzzle for a monkey to climb. Vicuñas *(right)* are the smallest of all camels. Weighing about ninety pounds and standing less than three feet tall, vicuñas live at high altitudes. These animals communicate by signaling one another with body postures and ear and tail placement, along with vocalizations of a high-pitched whinny that alerts the herd to danger. Once hunted to near extinction for its fleece, the protected vicuña is slowly increasing in number.

# THE PEOPLE

## The Ancient Aymara and the Modern Chileans

**H**unters, first entering Chile from the north, formed settlements around 13000 to 10000 BC. Unlike the indigenous peoples of Central America or other parts of South America, Chilean societies did not establish lasting civilizations or form an empire. Most people lived in small settlements or traveled as nomads. Archaeologists have unearthed relics from many ancient groups that long ago vanished or merged with other cultures.

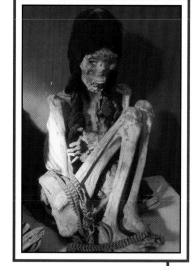

In the dry north, artifacts are better preserved than in the south. Among the most fascinating peoples in the region were the Chinchorro, who lived along Chile's northern coast from about 7000 until 1500 BC. They mummified their dead in an elaborate procedure, removing the brain, organs, and some bones and adorning the body with a sculpted mask and a wig. The oldest mummy dates to 5000 BC, some 2,000 years before the Egyptians began to mummify their dead.

Europeans, in expeditions from the north and the south, made the first contact with Chilean natives. In 1520, Portuguese explorer Ferdinand Magellan (c. 1480–1521) sailed around the tip of South America and traveled along Chile's coast. Spanish conquistador Diego de Almagro (1475–1538) descended through the Peruvian Andes in 1535. He explored the Central Valley in an unsuccessful search for gold.

This document (*left*), signed by Spanish conquistador Pedro de Valdivia in 1541, established Santiago as a Spanish settlement and the capital of Chile. Valdivia chose Santiago for its climate and the ease with which it could be defended. He hoped to find gold in the Marga Marga mines. Miss Chile of the Atacamanian culture (*above*) is a well-preserved mummy, approximately 1,200 years old.

This illustration shows Inca life around AD 1200. A powerful tribe, the Incas conquered weaker tribes to form the Inca Empire, which stretched along the western part of South America from what is now Colombia to Chile.

Lifestyles varied among the tribes that met the explorers. The Aymara lived in the Andes altiplano, herding llamas and alpacas and growing crops. The Diaguita were famous for their boldly patterned pottery, and the Atacameño farmed in the fertile parts of the dry north. On the coast, from the far northern region through to the Central Valley, the Chango hunted and fished.

During the fifteenth century, the Incas extended their rule throughout northern Chile. They built a network of roads to better enforce their authority. The Incas demanded tribute from conquered peoples and required that they practice the religious custom of sun worship.

When the Incas reached central Chile, they were stopped short by the warlike Mapuche, the largest of Chile's indigenous cultures. More than a dozen tribal groups ranged in the middle regions, varying in customs and lifestyles. Many cleared and farmed forest land, moving and resettling after the soil was depleted. They shared territory with a number of other tribes. The Picunche, "men of the north," farmed in the Central Valley, and the Huilliche, "men of the south," lived in the Lake District. The nomadic Pehuenche, Puelche, and Tehuelche of central Chile also resisted the Incan

This ceremonial headdress dating from AD 300 came from the coastal Atacama Desert. It is made of mesh net, vegetable dyes, and feathers.

# The People: The Ancient Aymara and the Modern Chileans

An illustration depicts an Ona Indian family at the doorway of a hut. The Ona Indians are now an extinct indigenous group. The last full-blooded Ona Indian died in 1974.

advance. Farther south, the Chono hunted, gathered, and fished among the harsh fjords and islands in the region near Chiloé.

Four groups inhabited the tip of the continent around the Tierra del Fuego. The Ona hunted on the plains and fished, and the Huash lived on the main island. The Yaghan and Alacalufe, the "men who travel in canoes," led a nomadic existence hunting seals and fishing. Some of the native peoples wore little clothing despite the harsh climate. They depended on fire for warmth even in their canoes. When Magellan traveled through the region, he named it Tierra del Fuego, meaning "Land of Fire."

Pedro de Valdivia (c. 1498–1554), a comrade of the conquistador Francisco Pizarro (c. 1475–1541), led the first Spanish settlers to Chile in 1540. He took with him only ten men and his mistress, Inés Suárez. More followers joined Valdivia as he traveled south. More than 150 settlers helped him establish Santiago in 1541. Valdivia later founded the cities of Concepción, Valdivia, and Villarríca. The Mapuche, whom the Spaniards called "Araucanians," resisted Spanish expansion south of the Bío-Bío River.

They might have yielded to the invaders much more quickly had it not been for the wits and daring of a young warrior named Lautaro (d. 1557). He

A portrait, circa 1500, of Francisco Pizarro, who defeated the Inca Empire and claimed most of South America for Spain. Pizarro conquered more territory in South America than any other military leader and delivered the most riches to his country.

# Robinson Crusoe Island

In 1704, a surly Scottish sailor named Alexander Selkirk was abandoned by his captain on a deserted island of the Juan Fernández Archipelago in the Pacific Ocean. Selkirk survived for more than four years before being rescued by a British ship. Novelist Daniel Defoe wrote a fictional account based on Selkirk's experiences, about a

young man named Robinson Crusoe who was marooned after a shipwreck. In 1966, the Chilean government renamed this island Isla Robinson Crusoe. A neighboring island was named Isla Alejandro Selkirk. Today, 500 people live in the town of San Juan Bautista on Isla Robinson Crusoe. The scant number of tourists who make the trip to the island can visit Selkirk's lookout point, a high peak overlooking both sides of the island. "Robinson" is a popular name among the men of the island!

The United Nations Educational, Scientific and Cultural Organization (UNESCO) has declared Isla Robinson Crusoe a reserve for its indigenous wildlife.

lived among the Spanish as a prisoner, handpicked by Valdivia as his page. After a year, Lautaro escaped. He returned to the Mapuche with expertise in horseback riding, weapons, and combat gleaned during his captivity. The Mapuche elected him to

A statue of Pedro de Valdivia stands in front of town hall in the Plaza de Armas, Santiago's historic center, where a fort was built in 1541 to house the city's first settlers. Valdivia established Santiago in the traditional Spanish checkerboard style, which is still apparent today in downtown Santiago.

become a leader in the fight against the Spaniards. In 1553, Mapuche forces began pushing northward, killing Valdivia and overwhelming his troops in one of the first battles. They achieved success during the next four years, almost reaching Santiago. Their fortunes changed when a member of another indigenous tribe killed Lautaro and the Spanish beat the Mapuche back to the Bío-Bío. The Mapuche continued to defend their land until the nineteenth century. The Spanish easily defeated most other indigenous tribes.

Fewer colonists came to Chile than to the rest of Latin America. They were kept away by Chile's geographic isolation, lack of gold or wealth, and the ongoing conflicts with the Mapuche. Nonetheless, the Spanish colony took root and grew steadily through the seventeenth and eighteenth centuries.

The first settlers received vast land grants called *encomienderos*, worked by an indigenous group called the *encomienda*. The Catholic Church and government intended that landowners educate workers and convert them to Catholicism. In reality, the wealthy often used the encomienda to create an unlimited supply of forced labor. Many native peoples died under brutal conditions imposed by the wealthy Spanish settlers. The indigenous population of the country decreased drastically as a result of the deprivations forced on them by the Spanish, diseases brought by the Spanish, loss of land, and war. With the decline of the indigenous workforce, the next

This map, circa 1600, shows the Strait of Magellan, explored by Ferdinand Magellan in 1520. Magellan sailed from Spain in 1519 in search of a trade route to the Spice Islands through the New World. As he moved south off the coast of South America, he discovered a passageway from the Atlantic Ocean to the Pacific Ocean that he named the Strait of All Saints, but it was later renamed after him. Magellan died shortly after his discovery. His crew crossed the Pacific to the Spice Islands and then sailed west back to Spain. Magellan's expedition took three years and was the first to circumnavigate the world.

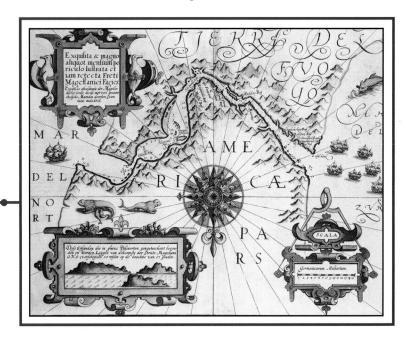

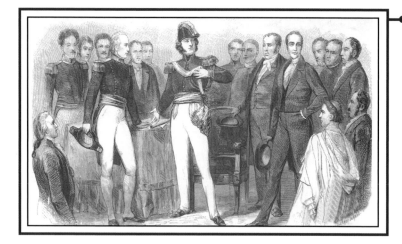

An illustration dated 1860 shows Bernardo O'Higgins renouncing his position as the leader of Chile in 1823. Although, he ruled as a dictator, he established a republic government and a Chilean navy, as well as libraries, courts, and hospitals. He implemented many social and educational reforms.

generation of landowners set up self-sufficient *haciendas* or *latifundios*. The workers on these large semifeudal estates were mestizos and the remaining native peoples. Mestizos had mixed native and Spanish blood.

The character of the ruling class also changed as time passed. The *criollos* were the descendants of the original Spanish settlers. They began to feel more loyalty toward Chile than to the interests of the Spanish rulers across the ocean.

In 1808, French emperor Napoléon Bonaparte (1769–1821) invaded Spain. In many Latin American countries, nationalists took advantage of the chaos within the ruling class. Independence movements gained strength. Chilean criollos revolted against the Spanish governor in 1810 and set up a native-born junta. Tensions rose between separatists and royalists, and Spain sent troops to quell uprisings. Bernardo O'Higgins (1778–1842), later called the Liberator of Chile, rose as leader of the Chilean nationalists.

O'Higgins was the illegitimate son of Ambrosio O'Higgins, an Irishman turned South American statesman, and Chilean-born Isabel Riquelme. He was educated in England and returned to Chile just as the nationalists ousted the Spanish. A firm supporter of Chilean independence, he took office in Congress and acted as a military leader. In 1813, Spanish forces moved to subdue the rebels and reestablish Spanish dominance. O'Higgins, who had become commander of the rebel troops, was defeated at Rancagua in 1814.

O'Higgins fled to Argentina and joined forces with the great Argentine general José de San Martín (1778–1850). Together, they led the multinational Army of the Andes to oust the Spanish. San Martín recognized that southern South America independence would not be secure as long as the Spanish viceroyalty in Peru held

# King of the Araucania

In 1859, young French lawyer Orelie-Antoine de Tounens heard about the noble Mapuche and took passage to Chile. On his arrival, he corresponded with the Mapuche *cacique*, or leader, Manil. When he crossed the Bío-Bío into Mapuche territory, this charismatic speaker enjoyed a stroke of luck. Native *machi*, or holy women, had predicted that a bearded white man would appear to lead the Mapuche. The southern tribes also accepted his claim to authority. Tounens declared himself the "King of the Araucania." He believed that the indigenous tribes, who had never been conquered by the Spanish, had a right to their own sovereign country. The Chilean government ignored Tounens and his nation. A year later, the native peoples planned an uprising. Tounens's servant betrayed him to the Chilean police. After a trial and six months in prison, Tounens was deported to France. He returned to South America three more times during his lifetime, making unsuccessful attempts to support Araucanian independence. Tounens died in France in 1878. Three years later, Chilean forces conquered the Mapuche and seized their land.

power. He set out to challenge the Spanish to the north. Spanish authorities officially recognized Chilean independence in 1818. San Martín's forces liberated Peru in 1820. Conflicts continued in Chile's southern regions until 1826, when Chilean forces defeated the last Spanish troops.

O'Higgins became the *director supremo* of the fledgling Republic of Chile in 1817. His rule was a virtual dictatorship. Many of the reforms he attempted alienated the powerful aristocracy. Pressured by this elite, the Catholic Church, and the military, O'Higgins resigned in 1823. He went into voluntary exile in Peru, never to return to Chile.

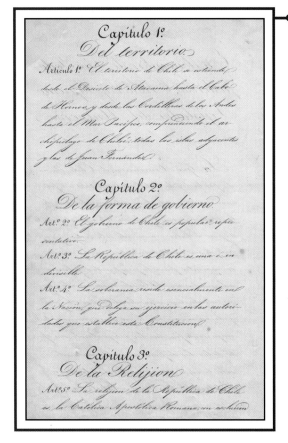

Capítulo 1°
Del territorio

Artículo 1°. El territorio de Chile se estiende desde el Desierto de Atacama hasta el Cabo de Hornos, y desde las Cordilleras de los Andes hasta el Mar Pacífico, comprendiendo el archipiélago de Chiloé, todas las islas adyacentes y las de Juan Fernández.

Capítulo 2°
De la forma de gobierno

Art° 2°. El gobierno de Chile es popular representativo.

Art° 3°. La República de Chile es una é indivisible.

Art° 4°. La soberanía reside esencialmente en la Nación que delega su ejercicio en las autoridades que establece esta Constitución.

Capítulo 3°
De la Relijion

Art° 5°. La relijion de la República de Chile es la Católica Apostólica Romana, con exclusión

Chile's constitution of 1833 put the government's power in the hands of the president and established a democracy.

The young republic saw many brief governments and unsuccessful constitutions in the subsequent decade. In 1830, Diego Portales (1793–1837), a conservative politician, emerged to stabilize Chile's political and economic affairs. Although never elected president, he controlled government policy until his assassination in 1837. His most lasting influence was the creation of a constitution in 1833 that established a centralized government and awarded the president near-autocratic powers. The Portalian Constitution limited government participation to wealthy landowners, merchants, the military, and the Catholic Church.

During the second half of the nineteenth century, nitrate and guano deposits were discovered and exploited in the Atacama Desert. Peru and Bolivia argued over Chile's land rights, sparking the 1879 War of the Pacific. Victorious, Chile acquired territory from both countries. The natural resources of these territories have contributed to the country's economy ever since.

José Manuel Balmaceda (1840–1891), elected in 1886, became the first president to attempt social reform. He proposed public works projects and an improved educational system, efforts that antagonized the conservative Congress. Political struggles escalated into a brief civil war. It ended in 1891 with Balmaceda's suicide and a strengthened Congress.

New tensions forced the government to address social issues. A huge disparity of wealth, education, and power existed between the elite and the majority of working-class

A suicide note left by José Manuel Balmaceda on September 18, 1891. Balmaceda, who was the leader of a liberal group, served as president of Chile from 1886 to 1891. During his term, quarrels with a conservative Congress escalated, and in 1891, a civil war broke out over the issues of presidential power. Balmaceda committed suicide rather than stand trial.

Carta

del Exc. Presidente Balmaceda

a los señores

Claudio Vicuña i Julio Bañados E.

Señores Claudio Vicuña i Julio Bañados E.

Santiago 18 de setl. de 1891

Mis amigos:

Dirijo esta carta a un amigo para que la publique en los diarios de esta capital, i pueda así llegar a conocimiento de todos, cuya residencia ignoro.

Deseo que vdes, mis amigos i mis conciudadanos, conozcan algunas verdades de actualidad i formen juicio acertado acerca de ellas.

El 28 de agosto despues de hecho el mando en el jeneral Baquedano, i de derecho terminó hoi la administracion el mandato que recibí de mis conciudadanos en 1886.

Las batallas de Concon i la Placilla determinaron este resultado. Aunque en Coquimbo i Valparaiso habia fuerzas considerables, estaban divididas i sin habia posibilidad de hacerlas obrar eficazmente para detener la invasion de los vencedores.

Con los ministros presentes acordamos llamar al jeneral Baquedano i entregarle el mando en algunas condiciones. Nos reunimos para este objeto en el jeneral Velasquez, i los señores Manuel A. Zañartu, jeneral Baquedano, i Eusebio Lillo, a quien habia pedido tuviera la bondad de llamar al señor Baquedano en mi nombre.

Quedó acordado i convenido, que el señor jeneral recibiría el mando, que se guardaría el órden público, haciendo respetar las personas i las propiedades; que los partidarios del gobierno no serian arrestados, ni perseguidos, i que yo me asilaría en lugar propio de la dignidad del puesto que habia desempeñado, para cuyo efecto se designó la legacion arjentina, a cargo del Exclentisimo señor Don José de Uribuna i decano a la vez del Cuerpo Diplomático, debiendo el jeneral prestar eficaz amparo al asilo i a mi persona, i aun de asegurar mi salida al estranjero.

Manifesté que en Coquimbo se podian reunir 6.000 hombres, i que en ese momento habia en Santiago 4.500 hombres

Augusto Pinochet was responsible for mass arrests and more than two thousand political assassinations. After Patricio Aylwin succeeded him as president, Pinochet commanded the army until 1998, when he was made senator for life. He was arrested in England later that year.

Chileans. The Chilean people began clamoring for a voice in politics. During the 1890s and the beginning of the 1900s, workers formed trade unions and clashed with government forces. The lower and middle classes formed political parties.

Chile remained neutral through World War I (1914–1918). After the war, socialist and communist parties grew stronger in Chile. Amid political and social conflict, a new constitution was drafted in 1925. It granted more power to the president and addressed social welfare issues.

For the next few decades, political turbulence continued to plague the Chilean government. The liberal and conservative factions split completely, leaving no common ground in their viewpoints. Although Chile officially sided with the Allies during World War II, the political events that occurred within Chile during this period had a more lasting effect on the country than the war itself. In 1970, leftist parties united under a coalition called the Popular Unity. Their candidate, the socialist Salvador Allende (1908–1973), narrowly won in a three-way race.

Once president, Allende instituted controversial social and institutional reforms during a time of economic crisis. He seized private land and nationalized many private enterprises. The state took control of banks, copper-mining companies, and privately owned monopolies. Right-wing parties and the U.S. government worked to prevent his reforms.

In 1973, General Augusto Pinochet (b. 1915) overthrew the government in a military coup, during which Allende perished. Pinochet took control as dictator. His forces tortured and killed thousands of his leftist opponents. Hundreds of thousands more fled Chile.

The military junta under Pinochet threw out the constitution, closed Congress, and outlawed political parties and labor unions. It initiated censorship of the media.

Demonstrators carry signs picturing people who disappeared after having been arrested by agents of Pinochet's government. In October 1998, London police, acting on a Spanish warrant, arrested Pinochet for human rights crimes committed in Chile during his seventeen-year rule. The Chilean Supreme Court stripped Pinochet of his immunity in 2000, and he was indicted and placed under house arrest in January 2001.

Pinochet suppressed any form of expression that questioned his regime, limiting civil rights, cultural movements, social programs, and political freedom.

Pinochet's drastic economic measures successfully revitalized the economy. However, a recession in the early 1980s led to large-scale demonstrations against the regime. In 1988, Chileans voted against extending Pinochet's term. Popular elections were held in 1989, and Patricio Aylwin (b. 1918) became president. Chile began a gradual return to democracy.

## Chileans Today

More than 75 percent of Chile's 15 million inhabitants are mestizos, of mixed European and native Indian ancestry. Most feel closer ties to European traditions than to their native heritage. The population is 90 percent European or mestizo and 10 percent Indian. Most immigrants have been European. Early colonists were Spanish, mostly of Basque origin. Subsequent waves of newcomers introduced elements from diverse cultures. Many Germans settled in the Lake District during the second half of the nineteenth century. Today, some communities still keep up German traditions and language. The British, Swiss, and French arrived at the same time. Newer immigrants include Italians, Jews, Koreans, and Middle Easterners.

Although Chilean society is not fractured by religious, regional, or ethnic conflicts, tensions and class barriers still exist. Rigid social classes dominate, topped by a wealthy,

*Santiago, 18 de Setiembre de 1925.*

*El Presidente de la República,*

*Por cuanto*
*la voluntad soberana de la Nación,*
*solemnemente manifestada en el plebis-*
*cito verificado el 30 de Agosto último,*
*ha acordado reformar la Constitución*
*Política promulgada el 25 de Mayo*
*de 1833 y sus modificaciones posteriores e*
*invocando el nombre de Dios Todopoderoso,*
*ordeno que se promulgue*
*la siguiente, como la*

---

Chile's constitution of 1925 was the second major charter in Chilean history. The 1925 constitution established the official separation of church and state, provided legal recognition of unions, and promised to care for the social welfare of citizens. Presidential and congressional elections were also staggered so that a chief executive could not immediately bring in a legislature.

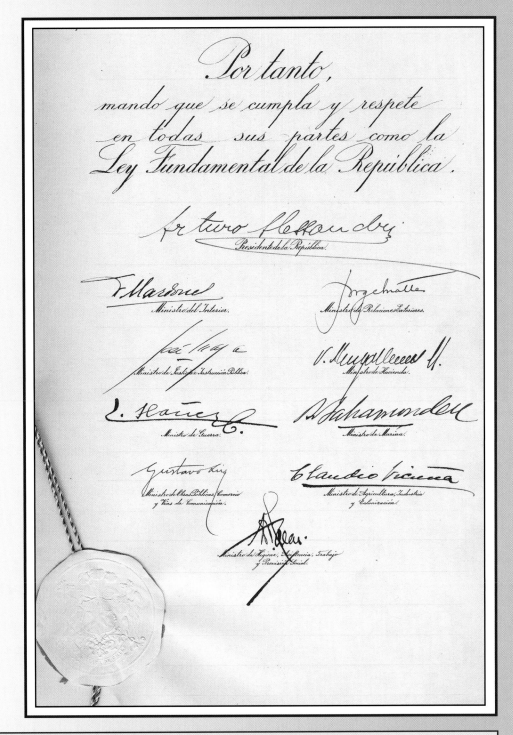

The last page of Chile's constitution of 1925 was signed by President Arturo Allessandri Palma and his cabinet members, who sought to equalize the power between the executive and legislative branches. The constitution divided the government into four branches: president, legislature, judiciary, and comptroller general, a position that judged the constitutionality of all laws requiring expenditure.

A historic picture shows Yamana Indians who inhabit the islands off the southern tip of Chile. Living in canoes, these indigenous people are called nomads of the sea. Well adapted to life in this harsh climate, they carry the minimal amount of equipment necessary for hunting, fishing, and daily life. They travel by canoe at night and build fires on gravel, turf, and stones in the bottom of their boats. Today the Yamana population is declining as the people are unable to adapt to sedentary life.

old-blood elite. Most people belong to a stable middle class, which is slowly becoming more socially mobile. More than 20 percent of the population are *pobladores*, the poor, living below the poverty line. The *retornados*, people who fled Pinochet's regime, returned with the reestablishment of democracy. They comprise a small but high-profile fraction of the population.

Few indigenous cultures survived the arrival of the Europeans. Many tribes merged with the Spanish and lost their cultural identities. The largest remaining group is the Mapuche. They number nearly a million. About 220,000 live on *reducciones*, or reservations, which make up a tiny percent of their original territory. In addition, 40,000 Aymara, some living traditionally as herders, live in northern Chile. The Huilliche and a few other small tribes still exist, mainly scattered in rural communities. Most of the Tierra del Fuego tribes are now extinct. Diminished by disease, the survivors were killed by ranchers

in the nineteenth century. Today, a large proportion of Chile's indigenous people live in poverty. Many have abandoned their cultural traditions.

A unique indigenous culture exists on Rapa Nui, or Easter Island, but few islanders retain memories of the forbears who created the moai (statues). By the time Europeans arrived, Rapa Nui's society was in decline, the result of environmental damage and internal conflicts. During the nineteenth century, slave traders captured many of the native peoples. New diseases ran rampant among the remainder, leaving only 110 survivors by the 1870s. Chile claimed Rapa Nui in 1888. The Chilean government was a harsh ruler, exploiting the land and labor of the indigenous population. In 1966, the government granted islanders full citizenship. It has since improved public services, hospitals, and schools and provided a new airstrip. Land rights and self-rule by the islanders remain highly debated issues.

In the Mapuche culture, a man could marry as many wives as he could support. However, the first wife was considered the first woman, or *unendomo*, who was the real house owner. All other wives of the family recognized the importance of her role. Mapuche women were responsible for knitting, the production of skins and leathers, pottery, and farming.

# THE LANGUAGES OF CHILE

## From Ancient Aymara to Modern Castellano

**3**

*Bienvenido a Chile*! If you are ever a guest in Chile, your host may greet you with this friendly welcome. Chileans speak Spanish, or Castellano, as they call it, referring to the Spanish region of Castile where the language developed. A Romance language, Castellano shares its roots with French. The Romance languages began to branch off from Latin in the ninth century. The family adopted the Latin alphabet, also used by English and other European languages. Spanish spread across the globe beginning in the sixteenth century as the conquistadors traveled far and wide, lured by riches and fame. Today, more than 400 million people in at least 43 countries speak fluent Spanish. It is the official language of most Central and South American countries.

Spanish spoken in Latin America is no longer identical to the Spanish of Spain. Dialects vary from one region to another, although Chileans have few problems communicating with other Spanish speakers. The differences arise mainly from accents and idioms, much like the variances between British English, American English, and Australian English. Chileans have a reputation for speaking very rapidly and leaving out consonant sounds near the ends of words.

When first opening a Spanish-language newspaper, a beginner will find a few unfamiliar markings. A symbol called a tilde above an *n* changes the pronunciation of

Rongorongo *(left)* is the hieroglyphic script of Easter Island. Engraved on wooden tablets, only twenty-one have survived. Scholars still disagree about the nature of the writing. However, scholars do know that it is read from left to right starting at the bottom left-hand corner. This outdoor magazine stand *(above)* is located in Valdivia. The official language of Chile is Castellano, a form of Spanish that is often spoken rapidly.

## Vocabulary

| | |
|---|---|
| **Hello** | Hola |
| | Buenos días (more formal) |
| **Good-bye** | Adíos |
| **Yes/No** | Sí/No |
| **Please** | Por favor |
| **Thank you** | Gracias |
| **Sorry** | Lo siento |
| **I don't know.** | No sé. |
| **What is your name?** | ¿Como se llama usted? |
| **My name is. . .** | Me llamo. . . |
| **I don't speak Spanish.** | No hablo español. |
| **Do you speak English?** | ¿Habla usted inglés? |
| **What time is it?** | ¿Qué hora es? |
| **Help!** | ¡Socorro! |
| **I'm lost.** | Estoy extraviado. |
| **How much does it cost?** | ¿Cuánto cuesta? |
| **How do I get to. . .?** | ¿Donde está. . .? |
| **House** | la casa |
| **Restaurant** | el restaurante |
| **Bathroom** | el baño |
| **Car** | el carro |
| **One** | uno |
| **Two** | dos |
| **Three** | tres |
| **Four** | cuatro |
| **Five** | cinco |

the letter. For example, in the word *mañana* (tomorrow), each *n* has its own sound: mah-NYAH-nah. Usually the stress falls on the last or second-to-last syllable of a word, but accent marks sometimes specify otherwise. *Sábado* (Saturday) is pronounced SAH-bah-doh, and *fotografía* (photograph) is foh-toh-grah-FEE-ah. Queries begin with an inverted question mark "¿" and end in a conventional question mark. Similarly, an exclamatory sentence begins with "¡" and ends in a regular exclamation point.

More consistent than in English, most letters have the same pronunciation in every context. Most vowels represent individual sounds rather than diphthongs, which combine vowel sounds. They are *a* as in mama, *e* as in mesa, *i* and *o* as in mosquito, and *u* as in boot. Some consonants have only subtle distinctions from English, but a few sound significantly different. The letter *h* is always silent, and *j* sounds like a slightly guttural *h*. The letters *ll* are pronounced like *y*, and *qu* sounds like *k*. Every *r* is rolled, and *x* and *z* are softer than in English, so *luz*, or light, is pronounced looss. The country of México is MEH-hee-koh.

Some grammatical situations in Spanish have no English equivalent. The word for "you" varies depending on the person being addressed and the circumstances. It may be either the formal *usted* or else the familiar *tú*. Most nouns are gendered in Spanish. In general, feminine nouns end in *a*, and masculine in *o*. Words require different articles or adjective forms depending on gender, for example, *la tienda* (the store) or *el marcado* (the market).

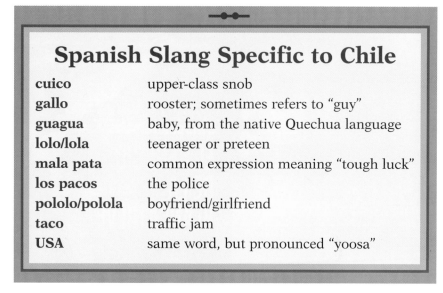

**Spanish Slang Specific to Chile**

| | |
|---|---|
| cuico | upper-class snob |
| gallo | rooster; sometimes refers to "guy" |
| guagua | baby, from the native Quechua language |
| lolo/lola | teenager or preteen |
| mala pata | common expression meaning "tough luck" |
| los pacos | the police |
| pololo/polola | boyfriend/girlfriend |
| taco | traffic jam |
| USA | same word, but pronounced "yoosa" |

Many English words come from Spanish origins, such as mosquito, banana, barbecue, renegade, ranch, and vanilla. Spanish also borrows from other languages. Chilean Spanish in particular takes words from indigenous tongues and the languages of minority settlers in the country. Thus, Chileans use some German words and phrases. Spanish has adopted many English words, especially terms related to technology and recent trends. Chileans think that *el internet*, *taxis*, and *VCRs* are *súper*!

## Other Languages

Chile was once home to a variety of indigenous languages. Like the native peoples themselves, these languages lost dominance after the arrival of the conquistadors. Some of these, such as the

PTO. MONTT 594
TEMUCO 968
SANTIAGO 1639
COPIAPO 2444
ARICA 3704

CON TRANSBORDO
EN CHAITEN

A road sign in Spanish indicates the distance in kilometers to Chile's cities and towns. Although Spanish is the official language of Chile, there are eleven different languages in the country, with nine living languages and two extinct ones.

# The Languages of Chile: From Ancient Aymara to Modern Castellano

These people of Rapa Nui, or Easter Island, are dressed in their native costumes. One theory about the origins of the Easter Islanders is that they are descended from Polynesians who discovered the island in AD 400. By the turn of the nineteenth century, the population of Rapa Nui natives was reduced to 111 people, the result of lost resources, disease, and slavery. However, since Easter Island became part of Chile in 1888, the population has risen to 2,000.

Yaghan language or the Kakahua tongue spoken by the Alacalufe people, have vanished completely or have only a few remaining speakers.

The principal surviving language is mapudungun, spoken by about 400,000 Mapuche. The tribe's name means "people of the land," from *mapu*, meaning "land," and *che*, meaning "people." The Mapuche never created a written version of their language. Catholic missionaries first transcribed the language using variations of European characters. Some Aymara speak their native language, Aymara, as do groups in Bolivia and Argentina, but most people consider Spanish their first language. A few thousand Huilliche in the south retain their Huilliche language.

The indigenous people of Easter Island, or Rapa Nui, speak a Polynesian dialect called *rapanui*. Among the mysteries of the island are the Rongo-Rongo tablets, wooden artifacts carved with now-forgotten hieroglyphics made up of stylized human figures, animals, plants, and geometric shapes. The islanders use their full name, *ko hau motu mo rongorongo*, meaning "lines of script for recitation." Oral history tells that only a few priests could read the texts, which are supposed to have held religious lore, records, and commemorative accounts. The last priests who understood the script died in the 1860s during slave raids or from the plague. Modern experts have yet to decipher their messages.

Although Chile's government is called a democracy, there are limits to freedom of speech and ideas. Under Chile's current constitution, censorship has been banned for all media except film. An agency bans films considered inappropriate for Chileans. Verbal expressions considered insulting to high-ranking state officials carry a prison sentence or a fine. Many of these restrictions are at the behest of conservative judges in office since the military governed Chile.

# CHILEAN MYTHS AND LEGENDS

## 4

Deep within the Andean forests of Chile, spirits await the call of sorcerers or the rituals of villagers. Across the country, the islanders of Chiloé warn their children to beware the *brujos*, or wizards. Older fishermen tell stories of seeing La Pincoya, the omen of an abundant catch. The stories, superstitions, and beliefs held by Chileans up and down their narrow country represent a living tradition in the daily lives of the nation's people. Young children learn lessons embodied within witty animal fables. Adults chuckle about how their ancestors were lured to Chile by a tall tale about a mythical city of gold.

## Mapuche Spirits

Much of Chile's folk tradition originated in Mapuche spiritual beliefs. In the Mapuche world, spirits and monsters stalked in the dark unknown, controlled by powerful human sorcerers. The creatures of Mapuche legend terrify both children and adults. Few want to walk through the forest and meet a *waillepen*, a large, carnivorous calf-sheep with shape-shifting abilities. Chilean lakes and waterways are sometimes said to be the homes of *shompalwes*. These demons grant good fishing to those who please them with offerings and bring chaos to the lives of those who give them nothing.

Moai, the stone carved monoliths made from volcanic rock *(left)*, are seen all over Easter Island in different shapes, sizes, and stages of completion. Scholars are unsure of what purpose the moai served, but evidence shows that they were carved by the ancestors of the present-day islanders. On average, the moai statues weigh eighty to ninety tons and range from three hundred feet to only several feet tall. Mapuche shamans *(above)*, called machi, are typically women who can communicate with the gods and serve as mediators between humans and spirits. Machi possess powers of good and evil to help the sick and dying.

On the slopes of the inactive volcano Rano Raku on Easter Island are hundreds of petroglyphs of the god Makemake, the great spirit of the sea, and a birdman, carved into hard, volcanic rock. The emblem of the Birdman cult was a crouching human profile with a bird head and beak. The Birdman festivities included a contest to obtain the first egg of the season from the off-shore islet. Winners of the contest were recorded in these rock carvings.

The Mapuche divide the spirit world into two sides: the *ngenechen* are good spirits associated with the forces of life and renewal, and various types of evil *wekufu* are associated with death and destruction. Powerful sorcerers called *kalku* control the wekufu, sending them out to punish enemies and commit wicked acts. Every kalku has a cherufe, a type of wekufu associated with heat or light. They are embodied in sacred objects such as pieces of volcanic rock or fragments of meteor. The Mapuche believe that the cherufe spirits came to Earth as cannibal giants disguised as comets. They are responsible for volcanic eruptions, and the kalku use them to control other evil spirits. Vampire spirits take the shape of winged serpents called *piwichens* that fly about at night, drinking the blood of the young. *Choñ-choñs* are vampire spirits in the form of winged heads. They sap the strength and health of anyone nearby. Victims of choñ-choñs can kill the evil spirit by plunging a knife into the ground when the creature cries out. Kalkus

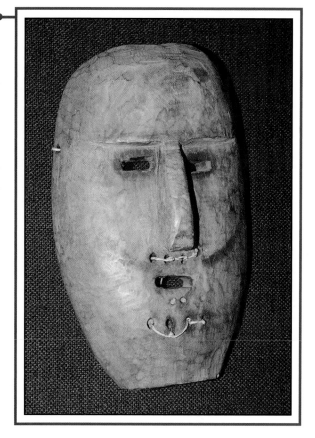

A traditional Mapuche face mask used in religious ceremonies

create *witranalwes*, or ghouls, by piecing together body parts of stolen corpses. These ghouls appear as glowing outlines in the night, luring travelers into danger. At other times, witranalwes manifest themselves as giants in normal Chilean dress, complete with ponchos and spurs! They attack their living victims from horseback.

The ngenechen spirits oversee growth and rejuvenation. The Mapuches revere them as gods and offer up prayers and sacrifices in return for favors. Guinechen, the master of the land, created the universe and all other spirits. He commands the entire spirit world, including the evil wekufu. The god Manquian was once a fisherman whose feet became caught in rocky crevices just off the coast. After a time he came to control the fish and watch over sailors. Küpuka fucha and Küpuka kushe are the god and goddess of abundance. Every year, communities hold prayer ceremonies called Ñguillatun directed by the *machi,* or shaman, in their honor. All villagers participate by singing and dancing, their faces painted a ceremonial blue and white. The machi erects a device facing east called a *rewe,* a "ladder to heaven" intended to communicate with the spirit world. In the past, animal sacrifices were made to Küpuka fucha and Küpuka kushe, but today the sacrifices are purely symbolic. After the ceremony, the whole village celebrates with a feast.

Most natural phenomena taking place within the Mapuche world are explained as the work of a spirit deity. Pillan fucha and Pillan kushe are the god and goddess of volcanoes and thunder. Antü fucha and Antü kushe, the god and goddess of the sun, work with Kügen fucha and Kügen kushe, the god and goddess of the moon. Together, they determine the length of the days.

An engraving on stone represents a large fish, possibly a tuna. Petroglyphs can be found all over Easter Island, especially hidden in meadows and by overgrown bushes. The symbols carved into stone typically depict images connected to fishing, such as sailboats, fish, octopus, and large seabirds.

The rugged, mountainous land inhabited by the Mapuche came about as the result of a contest between the good spirit Trey Trey and his evil nemesis, Kai Kai. They took the form of snakes, shaking the earth with their twisting. Kai Kai, attempting to get the better of Trey Trey, flooded the world, but Trey Trey built a great earth mound and escaped the rising waters. When the water receded, the mound remained behind as the Andes. As for Trey Trey and Kai Kai, the world still sometimes shakes with their eternal writhing.

Mapuche society navigates the potentially dangerous spirit world with the help of shamans. These individuals use magic for the protection and healing of the village. The most powerful and important are the machi, women who lead religious rituals and communicate with the spirit world. While they have a wide range of powers, other shamans specialize in one area. *Condeviecas* or *abagos* are soothsayers who make predictions by reading ears of corn or stones. *Achicos* can see the future through the behavior of animals. The *omus* are enchanters with the ability to heal using herbs. *Jambi camayocs* or *jambi camascas* drive evil spirits from the sick and cure poisonings. They lead double lives by also making poisons for their villages!

# Chiloé

The mysterious island of Chiloé, with a timeless tradition of storytelling and ritual, is home to some of Chile's richest folklore. Chiloé's residents speak in the hushed voices of the brujos, wizards who band together in a secret society that has remained on the

island for generations. Brujos grow in magical power by performing evil deeds. Tales explain that they must kill someone before being accepted as members. They hold meetings in caves guarded by an *invunche*, a magically malformed baby with crooked limbs and sealed orifices. Every night, the brujos take out the ghost ship *Calueche*, where the spirits of the drowned are picked out of the water. Once on board, the spirits are free to enjoy the never-ending party.

Other creatures stalk the island, some feared and some loved. The *trauco*, a malformed gnome with no feet, often attacks men walking alone at night. Older islanders still hold this strange little creature responsible for impregnating unwed women.

On the beaches, fishermen watch for the Pincoy and Pincoya, a merry pair who are half human and half fish. They dance on the beaches in the moonlight. If they are spotted facing the sea, then the next day's harvest will be good. The drowning sailor who finds himself washed up on the beach credits Pincoy and Pincoya for his rescue.

An Italian print portrays Captain Cook's visit to Easter Island. Upon his arrival, he found the inhabitants hospitable and willing to share what little food they had. According to Captain Cook's journal entries about the island, the islanders had a fascination with the crew's hats. When a small group of crew members explored the island, they found the huge stone monoliths toppled but all wore a "large Cylindric Stone of a red Colour worked perfectly round." One of the hats measured five feet across.

# Easter Island

The isolation and strange ruins of Easter Island, or Rapa Nui, convey a sense of mystery and wonder. Most of the island's original inhabitants died before their stories could be told, leaving scholars to puzzle out the details. Evidence shows that the island was first colonized sometime around AD 500, probably by both Polynesian groups and people from mainland South America. Some people have come up with bizarre, unlikely theories in recent years. They explain that the original inhabitants were descendants of ancient Egyptians, extraterrestrials, or survivors from the lost island of Atlantis!

One widely believed story suggests that the early Easter Island society was divided into two groups. The Long Ears had stretched, elongated earlobes, while the Short Ears had normal ears. The Long Ears were the social elite, served by the Short Ears until the Short Ears rose up in war against the Long Ears. Eventually, the Short Ears learned from a Long Ear traitor that the Long Ears were planning an attack that would wipe out the Short Ears forever. The Short Ears attacked first, setting fire to the Long Ears' defensive trenches. They killed all but the traitor by the light of the flames.

Though the legend may have some basis in fact, scholars now believe the names "Long Ears" and "Short Ears" are misinterpretations of the words *Hanau Eepe* and *Hanau Momoko*. Correctly translated, the two groups were the "Chubby People" and "Thin People." They maintain

A stone carving found at Easter Island depicts a birdman from the Birdman cult. In the seventeenth century, the focus of the Rapa Nui culture shifted from statue carving to the Birdman cult. The existence of the cult spanned from approximately 1680 until the last festival took place in 1866.

that the war was fought between Polynesian settlers, with more land and food, and poorer groups from South America.

Only the huge, brooding statues scattered about the island bore silent witness to the chaos of Easter Island's history. The giant stone figures, called moai, draw tourists from all over the world and fuel many of the theories about the original inhabitants. Once brightly painted and sometimes adorned with great stone hats, the figures are believed to represent either gods or dead chiefs. They served as a means of transmitting *mana,* or power, to a new family chief. When the Europeans first arrived during the 1700s, a few of the moai were still standing. By the end of the 1800s, a series of wars had devastated the island. Groups fought for control of the diminishing natural resources. All of the moai toppled.

A strange religion called the Birdman cult emerged during those

## Arturo Prat, Chilean Hero

Arturo Prat served as captain of the wooden battleship *Esmerelda* when the War of the Pacific broke out. In May 1879, the two largest ironclad battleships in the Peruvian fleet, the *Huascar* and the *Independencia*, trapped the *Esmerelda* in the Bay of Iquique. Prat refused to surrender and fought the Peruvian navy for nearly two hours before the *Huascar* rammed his ship. With only a handful of men, Prat leaped from the sinking *Esmerelda* to the *Huascar*'s deck. He fought on with his sword until he was cut down. His courage and gallantry revitalized the war effort. Arturo Prat became a hero overnight. Today, statues of the still-revered Prat occupy a spot in nearly every Chilean city and coastal town.

civil wars. The movement probably began as an attempt to distract the tribes from war. According to the beliefs of the Birdman cult, a birdlike god named Makemake created the universe. He brought the migratory sooty tern birds to the island every spring as a message of renewal. The village of Orongo was built high on the rim of the volcanic crater of Rono Kau specifically for the cult's rites. Believers moved to Orongo for the annual ceremonies. While there, they lived in egg-shaped stone houses, recited prayers, made offerings, and participated in fertility dances. The ceremonies culminated in a search for the first sooty tern egg of the spring. Finding the egg guaranteed a tribe's good fortune, and its chief became the birdman for a

year. The practice died out sometime in the 1870s, though the stone buildings and symbolic petroglyphs remain.

## Today's Chilean Tales

Even today, people believed to have special powers are treated warily, and supposedly haunted places are avoided. Stories about ghosts, animals, and the fantastic still bring on a shiver. The story of the City of the Caesars dates back to the days of the conquistadors. Greedy Spaniards would ask tribal chieftains where they could find gold in the country. The chieftains were eager to rid themselves of these unwelcome visitors, so they spun a tale about a fantastic city located far to the south and high in the mountains. The Spanish believed their accounts of a city built from European shipwrecks and filled with treasure. Explorers wandered all over the countryside chasing the improbable fantasy. Some Chileans today still dream of finding such a city in the most remote parts of the Andes and Patagonia.

Animal tales are commonly told throughout the country. Many of these come from Mapuche folklore and hold lessons for the young. Children often hear stories about quick-witted animals like foxes and squirrels outsmarting large carnivores, monsters, or bumbling humans. Other popular stories feature the mischievous Pedro Urdemales who makes his living by tricking the wealthy and foolish. In one tale, he steals an egg-shaped squash from a cruel farmer and sells it to a wealthy landowner. He claims that it is a mare's egg and that a swift racing horse will hatch from it. Pedro gained 5,000 pesos from the sale and made a clean getaway. The unlucky man dropped and broke his "mare's egg," which startled a fox nearby. The wealthy landowner is still chasing the fox he mistook for his prematurely hatched racing colt.

A painting by the contemporary Chilean artist Rocio Reyes-Cortez titled *Ngenenchen* depicts the Mapuche's supreme being and creator, Ngenenchen. Ngenenchen is part of what the Mapuche believe to be the divine family who punishes or supports man by expressing their powers of chaos, destruction, uncertainty, order, and harmony. The Mapuche believe that neither man, nor animal, nor insignificant insect could live without the grace of the great spirit, which encompasses all of the divine family. Mapuche closely relate to nature. Before using nature's offerings, whether it be animal or fruit, they ask permission and give thanks.

# CHILEAN FESTIVALS AND CEREMONIES OF ANTIQUITY AND TODAY

**5**

Chilean holidays and celebrations have origins in ancient tradition, national history, and modern commercialism. They reflect native lore as well as international influences. Before the Spanish colonized Chile, native peoples performed ceremonies paying tribute to the spirits. Many of these practices came to an end when Christianity spread through the population.

Today, religious feast days make up half of the official holidays despite the separation of church and state in 1925. But traditions from pre-Christian days still remain within the Catholic practices that replaced the old religion. Dances, music, costumes, and ceremonial rites that take place on some church holidays evolved from ancient rituals. Modern trends have also affected some holidays. It is common to see Santa Claus spreading Christmas cheer in the larger cities, sweltering under his heavy costume in the summer heat!

## Religious Feast Days

Easter Sunday, the day Christians believe Jesus Christ was resurrected from the dead, is the most important religious feast day for the Catholic Church. The Aymara and other northern Chileans anticipate Lent, the forty days

Santa Claus *(left)* is as popular in Chile as he is in the United States. Children open some presents on Christmas Eve and the rest on Christmas morning. Homes are decorated with a Christmas tree and a nativity scene. The holiday ends on January 6, the day of the Epiphany. The Fiesta de la Candelaria, Candlemas Feast *(above)*, commemorates the purification of the Virgin Mary forty days after the birth of Christ. In Copiapo, the Virgin Mary is honored as the patron saint of the miners. Every year a group calling themselves Chinos carries her statue in a procession. There are religious dances during the two-day celebration that bring together local folklore and the Catholic religion.

On December 8, 1854, Pope Pius IX declared that the Virgin Mary was exempt from all stain of original sin. That day has since been known as the Feast of the Immaculate Conception. In Lo Vasquez, a pilgrim wears a crown of thorns, representing Christ's final hours on this feast day.

that precede Easter, with a vibrant carnival on Shrove Tuesday. Palm Sunday, the Sunday before Easter, marks the beginning of Holy Week. During this week, some families attend daily church services. Communities hold prayer meetings, observe the Stations of the Cross (stations signifying the events in Jesus Christ's last days on Earth), make processions, and participate in other religious celebrations. Activities peak on Good Friday, marking the day Jesus was crucified. On Easter Sunday, families attend mass and spend the day together. Some hold an Easter egg hunt, a tradition borrowed from Chileans of German descent. A week after Easter is Cuasimodo. A priest in a horse-drawn carriage or on a float leads a

The festival of Domingo de Cuasimodo, celebrated the Sunday after Easter in central Chile. People decorate their homes and wear colorful costumes. The day begins with mass and a procession led by a priest. People follow, shouting "Viva Cristo Rey!"

procession through his community accompanied by *huasos*, or Chilean cowboys, and bicyclists.

Many Chilean religious feast days incorporate elements from indigenous animist rituals that celebrate inanimate objects. For example, on May 3, Santa Cruz de Mayo, Chileans honor the Christian cross. In some regions, celebrations include the sacrifice of a llama.

In mid-July, more than 40,000 believers gather at the village of La Tirana for a religious festival. The tale behind the celebration dates to the 1500s. An Incan princess, daughter of a high priest of the cult of the sun god, led a band of warriors in rebellion against Spanish conquistadors. For her military prowess, she gained the fearsome title La Tirana de Tamarugal, the tyrant of Tamarugal. One day, her men captured a Spaniard named Vasco de Almeyda. La Tirana fell in love with him, and she converted to Catholicism. She tried to impose Christianity on her followers, but they felt betrayed and killed the couple. Years later, a priest found her grave marked by a cross. When he heard La Tirana's tragic story, he had a church built at the site honoring the Virgin del Carmen, the Virgin Mary. Pilgrims attending the festival pay respect to the Virgin del Carmen, Chile's patron saint. Highlights include the performances of masked, costumed dancers. Women play the part of virginal maidens, and men represent devils. Activities continue for two weeks in a carnival atmosphere.

All Saints' Day and All Souls' Day on November 1 and 2 offer a solemn contrast to La Tirana. Chileans attend memorial church services and visit cemeteries to pay respect to the dead. On December 8, Immaculate Conception, many Chileans make the 53-mile (86-km) pilgrimage from Santiago to the Sanctuario de la Virgen de lo Vasquez, a small shrine between Valparaíso and Viña del Mar. Some carry crosses or holy objects; others crawl the last length to the shrine.

Households put up Christmas trees and other decorations on Christmas Eve. Families gather for an enormous late-night meal after which children open gifts. Some attend *misa del gallo*, midnight mass. Christmas is often a beautiful summer day perfect for picnics at the beach or *asados* (barbecues) with family and friends. Holiday treats include *pan de pascua*, a Christmas fruit bread, and *cola del mono*, "monkey's tail," a spiced and spiked coffee drink.

## Celebrations and Traditions

In February, Viña del Mar holds the weeklong Festival Internacional de la Canción, or International Song Festival. This extravaganza attracts musicians and fans across Latin

# Independence Day

On September 18, 1810, Chile took the first steps toward independence from Spain. Today, that date marks Fiestas Patrias, Chile's Independence Day. As it is also the unofficial beginning of spring, Chileans throw themselves enthusiastically into the festivities.

Dance pavilions, called *fondas*, spring up in empty lots and country fields. Parties last long into the night. Everyone dances the *cueca* and indulges in wine and empanadas, a favorite national food.

Children fly kites and the more competitive take part in contests. Kite strings are coated with pulverized glass, and the contestants try to cut other kites loose, until only the winner still has a kite in the air. The following day is Día del Ejército, or Armed Forces Day. A military parade in full uniform marches through Santiago's vast Parque O'Higgins.

America. Thousands purchase tickets far in advance, while others catch every minute of TV coverage that is broadcast around the world. Besides featuring well-known artists, it is a competition for lesser-known performers vying for the Gaviota (seagull) trophy.

May 21, Navy Day, commemorates the 1879 Battle of Iquique, which took place during the War of the Pacific. Chile lost the battle, but the bravery of Chilean hero Arturo Prat revitalized patriotism among the people. This day also marks the opening of Congress, and the president gives the state of the nation address. October 12, Dia de la Raza, was first initiated in Spain during the rule of Francisco Franco (1892–1975) but was discontinued after his death. Chileans still recognize the holiday. Also known as Hispanism Day or Columbus Day, it honors both their Hispanic

and native heritage. In November, the Mapuches and other indigenous peoples gather for Feria Indígena Cerro Huelén in Santiago, where they celebrate their cultures and hold a market.

Children celebrate birthdays much like in the United States, anticipating the day for weeks and throwing parties with presents and cake. But Chileans get to celebrate once again on their saint's day. Most Chileans are given names of Catholic saints who are recognized on a particular date. On the feast day of their namesake saint, they invite family and friends for a gathering much like a birthday party.

The Day of the Dead festival in Chile honors the dead and celebrates life. This holiday originated in Mexico from the combination of rituals dedicated to the Aztec war god and the Christian holiday of All Hallows' Eve. Today, people celebrate this day on the first two days of November. Festivities include visits to grave sites to decorate headstones with flowers and to bring food offerings.

# THE RELIGIONS OF CHILE THROUGHOUT ITS HISTORY

**6**

Catholicism is Chile's primary religion. Since the arrival of Spanish conquistadors in 1535, the Catholic Church has been present as a driving force in Chilean society. The church exerted a profound influence on Chile's history, even as tumultuous, political upheavals brought change within the church itself. Ever adapting to new situations, the Catholic Church has managed to grow and thrive. It has kept abreast of each new political phase and helped to steer the nation. Today, other faiths compete with Catholicism for Chileans' religious devotion.

## Early Catholicism

When Pedro de Valdivia claimed Chile for the Spanish Empire in 1540, he was also claiming it for the Catholic Church. Catholicism being the state religion of many European countries, the Catholic Church held close ties to many governments. It often influenced the outcome of world events. The Spanish conquest of new territories meant further expansion of the Catholic world. For its part, Spain received the church's sanction for its activities in Chile.

The church began missionary work in Chile in 1541, using the settlement of Santiago and its surrounding region as a base. Pedro de Valdivia established trusteeships for his followers. He granted them land and power. They were allowed to claim

The Shrine of Lo Vasquez *(left)* is dedicated to the Virgin Mary. Each year Chileans make the pilgrimage to honor her here. On December 8, they celebrate with the Feast of the Immaculate Conception. Plaques *(above)* thanking Saint Terese de los Andes outside a church dedicated to her in Calle Large, Los Andes. Saint Terese de los Andes was Chile's first saint.

tribute from the native peoples in exchange for teaching them about Christianity. The tribes often could not pay the high tributes set by Valdivia's trustees and were forced into hard labor. Very few indigenous people converted through this method. Instead, they often revolted against the cruelty of their teachers.

Franciscan missionaries arrived during the 1560s, hoping to convert Chile through gentler methods. They began their work in the north. The Franciscans built churches, abbeys, and missions to house any new followers.

Missionaries from the Jesuits arrived around 1600. Jesuit craftsmen of all descriptions aimed to civilize the native peoples and bring them into the church fold through education. They placed special emphasis on the importance of the patron saints, explaining them as a parallel to the spiritual world of the tribes. The Jesuits worked to improve the lives of the indigenous peoples. During the 1670s the Jesuits won the right to free any enslaved native person who had converted to Christianity. The influence of the Jesuits spread across the country. In 1767, however, the Spanish forced out the Jesuits for protecting the native population and organizing them into religious communities.

## A Catholic Nation

Catholicism dominated the settled regions of Chile by the turn of the nineteenth century. Missionaries still worked to convert the isolated northern regions and the territory of the fiercely independent Mapuche to the south. Otherwise, the church stood as the country's most influential cultural and political institution.

A priest offers the Sacrament during the Festival of Domingo de Cuasimodo *(above)*. Catholicism is the predominant religion in Chile. During the regime of General Pinochet, the Catholic Church played a key role in protecting the human rights of Chilean citizens. However, since the 1970s, the Catholic Church's influence in society has been decreasing because of the growth of evangelical churches. A church in Herradura *(right)* was designed by French architect Gustave Eiffel in 1889. It was built in France and shipped in pieces to Chile.

People walk toward a church built in honor of Saint Terese de los Andes. The church was built to hold her body and is the most popular Catholic sanctuary in Chile. At the beginning of March 1920, Sister Terese announced that she would die in a month. On April 2, Good Friday, she fell seriously ill with typhoid fever. She died ten days later. A few days after her death Father Julian Cea proclaimed that, "she will shortly perform miracles." Many young people look to Saint Terese de los Andes for guidance in living a Christian way of life.

The church supported Spain during Chile's sixteen-year war for independence. This stance caused some of the native-born criollo leaders to distrust the church. As Chile gained independence in 1818, the new Chilean government began looking for ways to limit the church's power yet still keep it as an ally. The government limited salaries for the clergy and confiscated church property in 1824. The Portalian Constitution of 1833 confirmed the close relationship between church and state. This document refused to recognize the civil rights of other religions.

At this point, the Catholic Church depended on the wealthy elite who controlled the country. The government approved all church administrative decisions in return for public gifts. This system was called the *patronato*. The church exchanged money and favors for the political support of Chile's Conservative Party. During elections, the church backed those politicians who were willing to make

## Mary and Peter

Catholic missionaries to Chile once worked to educate indigenous Chileans about the Catholic saints. They hoped that stories of their fantastic lives would appeal to new converts used to living in a world of spirits and magic. The Virgin Mary and Saint Peter made the deepest impression upon the Chilean people. Worshiped as the Virgen del Carmen, Mary is popular throughout Chile. Shrines devoted to her can be found all over the countryside. Oddly enough, she is the official patron saint of the Chilean armed forces. Desperate people prayed to her for mercy during the military dictatorship.

Saint Peter, or San Pedro in Spanish, revered along the coast, is the patron saint of fishermen. On June 29, the village of Horcón celebrates the festival of San Pedro. Villagers decorate buildings and boats and join in music and dancing. At the ceremony's culmination, an image of Saint Peter is placed in a boat and rowed around the bay to bless the waters and guarantee a bountiful harvest. On the island of Chiloé, the festival of San Pedro ends with villagers dumping a life-sized statue of Saint Peter into the ocean!

large donations. It would only allow congregation members to vote for certain parties. The poor and middle-class members of society became either indifferent or resentful toward the church. They viewed the institution as corrupt.

On the evening of Holy Friday in Chile, a procession winds through the streets of a small village near Chuquicamata. The image of Christ on the cross is carried as men and women dressed in mourning follow bearing lit candles.

## Reforming the Church

Between 1860 and 1935, the Radical, Democratic, and Liberal Parties attacked church privilege. These groups, known as the Liberal Alliance, worked to erode the power of the Catholic Church and its hold over the poor. In 1865, it became legal for members of all faiths to worship publicly and establish their own schools. Further reforms during the 1870s and 1880s took graveyards and civil records out of church hands. Civil weddings became the only recognized form of marriage.

The church and the state officially separated in 1925. Church leaders worried about a sharp decline in attendance by poor and middle-class members. They began severing political ties with the Conservative Party. Ritual celebrations and processions became common and attracted more people to the church. A group called Chilean Catholic Action, formed in 1931, served as a voice for social change and humanitarian causes. Members of this and other groups worked closely with the poor, helping to educate them and direct them toward better lives. Priests from other

In the Atacama Desert along the Panamerican Highway is a shrine of the Virgin Mary. She is revered throughout the country and is the official patron saint of the Republic of Chile, the Chilean army, and the Chilean navy.

countries volunteered for duty in Chile's slums and poor rural districts. They encouraged Chilean priests to do the same.

Catholic influence steadily increased among the poor through humanitarian projects. The upper classes saw this new social Christian movement as a threat to their power and privilege. During the early 1960s, the Catholic Church held a series of meetings of international church figures and thinkers. They called the conferences the Vatican II. It affirmed the Catholic Church's commitment to the poor and to humanitarian purposes throughout the world.

In Chile, the military coup of 1973 forced the church to take on a new role. It became clear that a return to democracy would be very slow. The church moved to establish a network of social welfare programs to replace those dismantled by the Pinochet dictatorship. Under the leadership of Cardinal Raúl Silva Henriquez (1907–1999), the church became one of the largest opposition groups within Chile.

In 1976, Silva established an organization called the Vicariate of Solidarity as an official ministry of the Archdiocese of Santiago. The Vicariate developed popular organizations meant to build solidarity and community and to help people in times of crisis. Health clinics and hot-lunch programs were established for the poor. Priests alerted their congregations to possible arrests, firings, and disappearances. Church officials donated money to the resistance press and helped farmers form cooperative organizations. The social programs developed under Silva reached many people previously disillusioned with the church. Weekly and monthly mass attendance increased, along with involvement in church organizations.

## Catholicism Today

The Catholic Church is one of the most powerful institutions in the nation. Seventy-nine percent of Chileans belong to the Catholic faith. More poor people attend mass regularly than in the past. They are still outnumbered in most congregations by the urban upper and middle classes. But the church's influence has declined since the late 1970s and early 1980s. Other faiths have begun attracting followers.

The Catholic Church plays a role in the average Chilean's life from infancy. At the age of six months, the child is baptized in a quiet family ceremony held at the parents' parish church. In rural locales, the ceremony takes on a more festive atmosphere. The entire community celebrates with food and drink. Children officially become church members around the age of eight, when they take their first Communion. The church remains present in the lives of nearly all its members through saints' days, weddings, feast days, and funerals. Regular services include Wednesday and Sunday masses, along with weekly private confessionals.

## Other Faiths

Other faiths began taking root during the mid-nineteenth century, with the arrival of German and British settlers. They wanted to practice their own forms of Christianity legally. Today, the fastest-growing religions in Chile are evangelical Protestant denominations. The Mormons and the Jehovah's Witnesses have also expanded greatly since the 1970s. These faiths have spread among the poor and in rural areas where the influence of the Catholic Church is more limited. Judaism and Islam are also present in Chile, mostly in small, tightly knit communities around the larger cities.

The spread of Christianity throughout Chile eliminated many beliefs of the native peoples, though a few are kept alive within remote communities. Some of the northern Aymara practice an animistic religion based on the idea of a natural balance between good and evil. The focal points of their faith are two gigantic volcanoes, Parinacota and Pomerape. The volcanoes, seen as powerful gods, receive attention in festivals and ceremonies intended to bring good fortune throughout the year.

The Mapuche faith is based on the belief in a perfect balance between good and evil. Their religion is animistic, giving powers and properties to natural phenomena.

A Mapuche woman plays the *kultrún*, a percussion instrument made by stretching leather over the top of a wooden bowl. The machi, the Mapuche spiritual healer, plays a kultrún during prayers and religious ceremonies. They believe that the kultrún enhances the machi's supernatural powers.

The Mapuche do not build houses of worship. Instead, they assign spiritual meanings to geographic features, plants, and animals. Good energy is concentrated in the east and is associated with life and renewal. Negative energy emerges as malicious spirits wreaking havoc upon the Mapuche world. Beliefs of individual communities within the Mapuche tribe vary depending on their geographic location. People in fishing villages place a greater spiritual emphasis on the water and aquatic life. Those in the Andes focus more on particular mountains and forest creatures.

Women called machi are believed to have the power to communicate with positive spirits. They lead ceremonies invoking them for the benefit of the village or tribe. Other important figures in the Mapuche faith are shamans and healers. The magic of the shamans also involves interaction with the spirit world, though they cannot communicate directly with the spirits. Their magic is often limited to foreseeing the future. The healers are able to drive out evil spirits by causing sickness with a combination of herbs, potions, and incantations. Though most Mapuche claim at least a surface belief in Christianity, their rituals remain vital to preserving their original culture and way of life.

# THE ART AND ARCHITECTURE OF CHILE

**7**

hile's vibrant culture reflects both contemporary and traditional influences. Recent political events as well as Chile's unique heritage have shaped its art and architecture. Painters and sculptors take their places beside indigenous metalworkers and weavers in the Chilean art world. The film and theater communities, stifled during the Pinochet regime, are once again healthy and growing. The country's eclectic architecture ranges from ancient fortresses to modern high-rise buildings.

## Pre-Columbian Treasures

Indigenous peoples crafted many items that have survived for hundreds of years. The best-preserved relics come from the northern part of Chile, particularly from the Atacama Desert. Tombs located in the desert and in dry Andean caves have yielded many clues about the past. Archaeologists working at such sites have unearthed artifacts ranging from woven baskets and clothing to weapons and pottery.

Relics created and used by ancient Chilean tribes extend far beyond stone tools and pottery. Geoglyphs are some of the most visible and spectacular sites found in the Atacama Desert. These massive designs were created when people placed dark stone and earth on hillsides or scraped the ground to reveal lighter soil.

A weaving *(left)* created by the Mapuche can be found in the Museum of Pre-Columbian Art in Santiago. In the Mapuche culture, weaving and other arts are especially important because the symbols and patterns often replaced writing. A jar *(above)* was created by the Diaguita culture, a group of indigenous people who lived in the mountainous interior of Chile. The Diaguita tribe had a seminomadic lifestyle and was one of Chile's most advanced cultures.

They adorn the landscape throughout the driest desert in the world. Visible for many miles, geoglyphs may have served as road markers for ancient caravans. Petroglyphs are designs carved and painted into stone walls near riverbeds or rocky outcrops. They are smaller in scale and far less elaborate than the geoglyphs, but they are also quite common in the Atacama Desert.

# Chilean Art

Early Spanish colonists had more pressing concerns than the development of a Chilean art tradition. Those interested in art brought paintings and sculpture from Europe or neighboring colonies. What little art they did create consisted mostly of religious statues and paintings meant for the church. Many of Chile's older churches, such as the Convento y Museo de San Francisco, feature religious portraits, carvings, and stained glass as part of their structures.

The establishment of a nationalistic art movement began in the mid-nineteenth century. Artists followed European forms while addressing Chilean themes. Portrait artist Jose Gil de Castro (1785–1841) gained fame for his portrayals of well-known subjects. His most widely recognized work is a portrait of Chilean hero Bernardo O'Higgins in 1824. Gil de Castro's painting shows the exiled former president still confident and defiant a year after resigning. Landscape painter and portrait artist Raimundo Monvoisin (1790–1870) worked in relative obscurity for much of his life. However, his oil-on-leather portrait of Carmen Alcalde Velasco de Cazotte (1843) draws the attention of modern viewers. It stands out for its sharp contrasts between pale skin, dark hair, and a deep red background.

La Academia de Pintura, or the Chilean Academy of Painting, was founded in 1849 to develop the talents of Chile's young artists. Art critics such as Pedro Lira (1845–1912), himself a

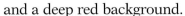
The title of this 1997 watercolor painting by Chilean artist Luis Guzman Molina is *Casa de la cordillera en Chillan*. Translated, this means "house in the mountains in Chillan." This painting depicts a wooden house that is characteristic of Chillan, an area south of Santiago. Molina is considered one of the best watercolorists in the world.

Roberto Echaurren Matta studied architecture and went on to become a master of surrealist painting. The surrealist movement, founded in 1924, focused on the expression of imagination as it is revealed in dreams. Matta's art has often been compared to science fiction.

painter, helped to define Chilean art movements. Lira brought national recognition of the art world to his country through columns and reviews.

European trends continued to influence Chilean art, particularly as impressionism became popular in the late nineteenth century. Later, abstract forms gained recognition in Europe and beyond. Chilean artists soon became internationally known as pioneers in contemporary art. Roberto Matta (1911–2002) is considered one of the original abstract surrealists. His art examines the interactions of the organic with the mechanical, in the belief that all forms are ultimately related. His *Birth of America* (1960) shows an assembly of strange beings surrounded by green and yellow lights on a field of blue.

Artists working during the Pinochet dictatorship often produced works showing violent upheavals and traumas in everyday objects and situations. Gonzalo Diaz (b. 1947) creates

Prints and paintings are for sale in the Plaza de Armas in Santiago. Art is very popular throughout Chile, both on and off the streets. The Museo Nacional de Bellas Artes in Santiago was founded in 1880 and is the oldest art museum in Latin America.

collages such as *La Lumberica* (1989), in which vivid brush strokes disrupt serene photographic montages. Alicia Villarreal (b. 1957) works with projectors and photographs in Montaña to show familiar objects disassembled and disarranged. A typewriter becomes a series of objects completely unrelated to each other. She systematically separates and photographs keys, rollers, and the machine's body itself. Anonymous artists made an even more lasting impact with murals. Their public works present the struggle toward democracy after years of oppression under the military dictatorship. The murals frequently adorn Chilean buildings, sometimes appearing overnight.

## Film and Theater

Prior to the 1973 coup, Chilean film was the most experimental and cutting-edge in South America. Alejandro Jodorowsky (b. 1930) received international attention in 1970 with his surrealistic *El Topo* (The mole). It takes the viewer on a ride through a nightmarish desert alongside the gunfighter El Topo and his young son. Miguel Littin (b. 1942) is perhaps the most acclaimed Chilean filmmaker. He first gained notoriety in 1969 with *El Chacal de Nahueltoro* (The jackal of Nahueltoro). The film provides a gripping depiction of the inescapable cycle of poverty and violence playing out in shantytowns and slums throughout Chile. Littin's most important work is the documentary *Acta General de Chile* (1986). Exiled from Chile since 1973, Littin slipped back into the country in 1985. His teams secretly filmed this account of oppression and misery under the military government.

Chilean film suffered greatly when Augusto Pinochet came to power in 1973. Film and art schools were shut down. Most filmmakers went into exile. Film censorship was finally lifted in 1997, though the recovery of the Chilean cinema has been slow. Cinematographers such as Gustavo Graef-Marino (b. 1965) have drawn the world's attention back to the Chilean film community. His 1994 film *Johnny 100 Pesos* drew raves for its portrayal of youthful middle-class bank robbers hiding out in a Santiago high-rise.

Chilean-born director and producer Miguel Littin *(far right)* was the head of Chile's film industry during the Allende government of the 1970s. After Allende's overthrow, Littin fled to Mexico, where he continued to work in exile. In 1985, he managed to reenter the country. His 1970 film *El Chacal de Nahueltoro* was his directorial debut and examined the underprivileged population of Chile. This documentary-style film re-creates a horrific event in Chile's history, a farm laborer murdering his wife and children. At the time, it was the most widely seen film in the history of Chilean cinema.

An Araucanian Indian woman sits at a loom. Women weave very large pieces of tapestry using a *witral* or vertical weave stool. In the Mapuche culture, weaving is exclusively a feminine trade, and only skilled weavers, called *duwekafe*, know the symbols hidden in colors and designs.

Chile has a long and proud theater tradition dating back to the construction of the Teatro Municipal in 1857. In the early twentieth century, the Chilean theater world split into two categories, public and private. The public companies continued performing traditional plays. Private groups began experimenting with free artistic expression and social commentary. The military dictatorship left most of the traditional public venues alone. Smaller independent stages and companies were either shut down or forced to mask their messages. Still, actors often risked arrest by performing short, anti-Pinochet sketches in public places.

Theater recovered from the dictatorship much more quickly than film. In 1993, Chile hosted the International Theater Institute Festival. Actors from all over the world came to participate in two weeks of plays and events. Today, small theater companies flourish in villages throughout the country. La Tropa is one of the best known. This three-person group is famous for its short, spontaneous performances in public parks. No one has to flee afterward.

## Traditions

Folk art practiced by the indigenous peoples still provides a livelihood for skilled artisans. Mapuche women weave warm and colorful ponchos, rugs, and blankets from the wool of sheep and alpacas. They derive the vivid colors from natural dyes. Silversmiths tool jewelry and other decorative pieces. They adorn them with etchings and semiprecious stones. Their finest works often feature a blue stone called lapis lazuli, found only in Chile and Afghanistan.

Ceramic workers use brilliant colors and distinct patterns on their ceramic bowls, platters, and other goods, which they fire by hand. The Diaguita people decorated ceramics in red, white, and black geometric patterns more than 500 years ago. Today, their work is the most imitated style in all of Chile.

Basket makers weave their products from a wide range of natural local fibers. The styles and materials used to weave baskets vary widely, depending on what type of reed or straw grows nearby. Chilean craftspeople display their work weekly at local markets, where savvy buyers can decide between a soft, waterproof poncho or lapis-adorned silver earrings. The Museo de Arte Popular Americano in Santiago displays folk art from both North and South America.

### Arpilleras

After the military coup in 1973, many women began quietly telling the stories of their missing loved ones through *arpilleras*. The word itself means "burlap," but came to stand for wall hangings sewn from scraps of cloth. Women collected the scraps themselves, or the church donated pieces of cloth to their projects. Some of the pieces re-create elaborate scenes from the lives of missing loved ones. Others express grief and frustration with only a couple of poignant words. Many were smuggled out of the country in order to show the rest of the world what life was like under a harsh dictatorship. Years after the return of democracy, arpilleras remain a popular folk-art medium of expression as well as an important legacy of Chile's history and culture.

## Architecture

Chile's most spectacular and enduring architecture dates from the late eighteenth and nineteenth centuries. Architects followed traditional European forms, giving cities an

In the Atacama Desert, a human figure is etched into Solitary Mountain. The world's largest geoglyph, it is 393 feet long. Chile's geoglyphs, representing people and animals, were created by removing dark pebbles to expose a lighter underlying soil. They are the only ones in the world to follow ancient caravan routes, which traveled east to west between the Andes and Pacific Ocean, and north to south, between the oases and desert. Archaeologists believe that the geoglyphs are about 2,500 years old.

Old World look. Most points of interest are located in the densely populated Central Valley.

To the north, few people live in the harsh desert. Those who explore the area can view the ruins of fortresses that once guarded indigenous territories. Pukara de Copaquilla is one of the best examples. Built in the twelfth century to protect vast terraced fields near the valley of Copaquilla, the fortress has recently been restored. Abandoned nitrate towns dot the Atacama Desert. The town of Humberstone was established as a national monument in 1970 and is open to visitors. A number of observatories take advantage of northern Chile's clear atmosphere. Some of the world's most powerful telescopes are located in this region. One of the telescopes in the Cerro Tololo Inter-American Observatory sports a thirteen-foot (four-meter) mirror!

Santiago is the nation's architectural epicenter, centered around the Plaza de Armas. Pedro de Valdivia established the plaza as a convenient place to store weapons

The Palacio de la Moneda on Santiago's Plaza de la Constitucion was once the residence for Chile's presidents. Although it stopped being a home in the 1950s, it is still the official seat of Chile's government.

when he founded the city in 1541. It served as Santiago's nucleus until the urban sprawl of the nineteenth century erased any earlier city planning. Today it encloses public gardens and sculptures. The Palacio de la Moneda was built in 1805 as the national mint. It later became the presidential palace. The 1973 coup nearly destroyed the building, but it has since been rebuilt.

The city boasts many excellent museums. The Museo de Santiago tells the city's story through an assortment of dioramas and models. The Museo Chileno de Arte Precolombino is housed in the beautiful old Royal Customs Palice. It maintains a large collection of artifacts collected from across Latin America.

Chile's oddest souvenir of the War of the Pacific, the Neptune Fountain, is displayed in Valparaíso. The fountain was taken from Peru in 1879. Featuring a huge statue of the Roman sea god, it serves as a centerpiece for the Plaza Victoria.

The Chilean government's legislative branch meets in the huge, defiantly modern Congreso Nacional building in Valparaíso. Completed in 1990, it was the last public works project of the Pinochet government. Legislators complain about its distance from the rest of the government in Santiago. There is talk of moving the legislature back to the capital and leaving the structure empty.

Chilean poet Pablo Neruda's favorite home, Isla Negra, rests on a rocky ocean headland not far from Valparaíso. It houses the Museo Neruda, a vast collection of the poet's belongings and memorabilia. His tomb overlooks the sea from Isla Negra's gardens, within range of the sound of crashing waves.

This arpillera represents friendship. On the left is a depiction of Santiago. The bright colors and charming figures made of fabric have an innocence that fuels the power of their message. During the regime of General Pinochet, arpilleras became protest banners calling for justice, freedom, and equality. The widows of men who "disappeared" sew and sell arpilleras to earn a small income for their families.

# Living at Home

The typical Chilean home varies from one region to another. Many factors decide the best type of housing for an area, such as the climate or a community's cultural traditions. In the hot, dry north, most people live in adobe houses with thick walls to keep interior rooms cool. People in the Central Valley region build Mediterranean-style homes with stucco walls. Their tiled, sloped roofs allow water to run off. German and Swiss settlers constructed European-style dwellings with steep, tiled roofs in the Lake District.

Traditional Mapuche houses are called *rukas*. They are usually thatched one-room homes with a central fire pit. A single doorway faces eastward, the direction in which good spirits live. Along the islands and coastlines near Chiloé, families dwell in mobile houses on wooden stilts called *palafitos*. To move them, people pull out the stilts and tow the structure by boat to a new location. One community was so accommodating to palafito residents that the mayor had streetlights installed in the water just offshore!

Modern high-rise apartment buildings dot the skylines of many Chilean cities. The finest provide homes for members of the upper and middle classes. Standing in stark contrast are the *casetas*, government-funded low-income housing. Chile began hiring contractors to build housing for the poor in 1906. The government itself began building housing with the establishment of the Housing Corporation in 1953. Pinochet decreased funding to less than half of the 1970 levels. He also increased the number of projects built each year. The government cut corners in order to save money. Many of the public housing units built during his dictatorship are falling apart.

In recent years, the government has tried to ease a growing housing shortage. It increased funding again after the dictatorship ended. The government still has a long way to go. People with no other choice make homes in hastily built shacks called *poblaciones*. Today, shantytowns of poblaciones crowd the edges of cities and large towns. They serve as reminders that Chile's housing problems continue.

# CANTO
## PRIMERO,

EL QVAL DECLARA EL
aßiento, y defcripcion de la Prouincia de
Chile, y eftado de Arauco, con las coftum-
bres y modos de guerra que los naturales
tienen: y aßi mifmo tracta en fumma
la entrada, y conquifta, que los
Efpañoles hizieron, hafta que
Arauco fe començo
a rebelar.

N O las damas, amor, no gentilezas
De caualleros canto enamorados,
Ni las mueftras, regalos y ternezas
De amorofos affectos y cuydados,
Mas el valor, los hechos, las proezas
De aquellos Efpañoles esforçados
Que a la ceruiz de Arauco no domada
Pufieron duro yugo por la efpada.

A                    Co-

# THE LITERATURE AND MUSIC OF CHILE

**8**

Chilean poet Pablo Neruda once wrote a lyric ode about a pair of socks. At first thought, it seems a strange concept. However, the expressive way in which Neruda wrote it compels readers to see the potential beauty of everyday objects. Of the five Latin Americans to win the Nobel Prize in literature, two were Chileans—Pablo Neruda and Gabriela Mistral.

During the second half of the twentieth century, a number of Chilean authors rose to international acclaim. Chilean authors have penned internationally acclaimed books. Many of these writers became famous during the presidency of Salvador Allende, but they were forced to either flee their country or risk torture and execution during the Pinochet years. Those who stayed behind now resent those who left.

Chileans consider themselves a nation of poets. Neruda and Mistral, their best-known poets, are deeply loved among the nation's people. The Chilean poetic tradition extends far into the nation's past, back to the days of the conquistadors. Alonso de Ercilla y Zúñiga (1533–1594) was a Spanish soldier fighting against the Chilean tribes when he penned the first epic poem in the Americas. He wrote "La Araucana" to honor the courage and spirit of the warriors he fought in Chile. The poet Andrés Bello (1781–1865) was born in Argentina, but spent half his life

Spanish poet soldier Alonso de Ercilla y Zúñiga wrote the first epic poem *(left)* in the New World titled *Canto primero de la Araucana*. In 1945, poet Gabriela Mistral *(above)* became the first Latin American woman to become the Nobel laureate in literature. The themes in her work addressed love, nature, sorrow, and recovery. She was also an educator, cultural minister, and diplomat.

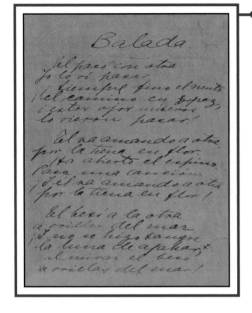

The title of the poem "Balada" means ballad. It was written by Gabriela Mistral. One of Chile's most famous authors, she is often referred to as *la divina Gabriela* (the divine Gabriela).

living in Chile, founding the Universidad de Chile. His works celebrate the beauty of nature and life in the countryside. A writer and scholar on many subjects, he is most famous for the two-part epic poem "Silvas Americanas" (1827).

Gabriela Mistral was the pseudonym of Lucila Godoy de Alcayaga (1889–1957). A schoolteacher from the town of Vicuña, she traveled throughout the world as an educator. She spoke eloquently for many social causes. Deeply affected by the suicide of a former suitor, she wrote poems that often addressed the topic of love and its many facets. Her best-known collection of poetry, *Desolación* (Desolation, 1922) is filled with sadness and deep longing for love. *Tenura* (Tenderness, 1924) speaks of the joy of loving all things. In 1945, she became the first Latin American, the first Chilean, and the first female poet to win the Nobel Prize in literature.

Pablo Neruda (1904–1973) was Chile's greatest and best-known poet. Born Neftalí Ricardo Reyes y Basoalto, he began writing poetry under the name Pablo Neruda at the age of sixteen. He published his first book of poems, *Crepusculario* (Twilight) in 1923. His 1924 volume, *Veinte Poemas de Amor y Una Canción Desesperada* (Twenty love poems and a song of despair), became a best-seller. He wrote freely in many styles. His verse expressed complex emotions, such as

Pablo Neruda is the most widely read Spanish American poet. At the age of twelve, he met Chilean poet Gabriela Mistral, who encouraged his writing. Neruda's first work, an article, appeared in 1917 in the magazine *La mañana*. In 1924, he gained international fame with his most popular work *Veinte Poemas de Amor y Una Canción Desesperada*.

the desire to become a voice for those unable to speak, as in "The Heights of Macchu Picchu" (1958). As noted earlier in this chapter, other works by Neruda focused on finding sublime beauty in simple objects such as a pair of socks in "Oda a los Calcetines" (Ode to my socks, 1961). A political activist, he often included progressive themes in his works. This won him a reputation as a poet for the common man. Neruda won the Nobel Prize in literature in 1971, while serving as the Chilean ambassador to France. He died of cancer just two weeks after the September 1973 coup, but the people he championed and inspired claim that it was really from a broken heart.

After Neruda's death, Chilean poets attempted to escape his shadow. They followed the example of Nicanor Parra (b. 1914). Parra created a form of expression that he dubbed "anti-poetry." Rather than express idle thoughts or personal pain, anti-poetry focuses on putting cultural and political commentary into verse form. Neruda himself praised Parra's collection *Poemas y Antipoemas* (Poems and antipoems, 1954) for the style and the progressive viewpoints expressed within. Like Neruda, Parra became an avant-garde icon among late-twentieth-century Chilean poets.

## Literature

Early Chilean authors began a long tradition of expressing their political views in their writing. Alberto Blest Gana (1830–1920) was

### The Morning Is Full

The morning is full of storm in the heart of summer.

The clouds travel like white handkerchiefs of goodbye, the wind, traveling, waving them in its hands

The numberless heart of the wind beating above our loving silence.

Orchestral and divine, resounding among the trees like a language full of wars and songs.

Wind that bears off the dead leaves with a quick raid and deflects the pulsing arrows of the birds.

Wind that topples her in a wave without spray and substance without weight, and leaning fires.

Her mass of kisses breaks and sinks, assailed in the door of the summer's wind.

—Pablo Neruda, 1924

one of Chile's earliest novelists. He focused on the human condition and a need for social reforms. He framed his ideas in historical novels set around the time of Chilean independence through the mid-nineteenth century. In works such as *Durante la reconquista* (During the reconquest, 1897), Gana mocks the upper classes as sinister and ridiculous. He contrasts them with roguish lower-class characters.

María Luisa Bombal (1910–1980) wrote early surrealist novels that explored the feminine consciousness. Her short story "El árbol" (The tree, 1939) was written to be read specifically to the music of Wolfgang Amadeus Mozart (1756–1791), Ludwig van Beethoven (1770–1827), and Frédéric Chopin (1810–1849). Each composer corresponds to a particular period of the lead character's life.

A number of talented Chilean writers began to emerge during the late twentieth century. Best known is Isabel Allende (b. 1942). Her *The House of the Spirits* (1982) is the second most widely read Latin American novel after *One Hundred Years of Solitude* by Gabriel García Márquez (b. 1928). Using Chile's military coup as a backdrop, Allende's work tells the story of an aristocratic family disintegrating in the midst of social upheaval. Some Chileans criticized her for fleeing the country in 1975 and then using its political troubles as a setting for her novel.

Isabel Allende's work combines harsh and realistic tones with the surreal in the tradition of magical realism, which is popular among many Latin American writers. Writing about political situations as well as the role of women in Latin America, she is considered a strong force in the feminist literary movement.

Most of Chile's celebrated contemporary authors left the country and became expatriates after the 1973 coup. Ariel Dorfman (b. 1942) first gained attention during the late 1960s as the coauthor of *How to Read Donald Duck* (1971). This work offers a scathing analysis of the pervasiveness of American culture. After leaving Chile in 1973, he wove themes of torture and repression into his acclaimed plays *Windows* (1982) and *Death and the Maiden* (1992).

Novelist José Donoso (1924–1996) focused on the contrasts between modern urban societies and an idealized traditional rural life. His best-known work, *The Garden Next Door* (1992), detailed the pain and isolation of an exile leaving Chile behind. Antonio Skármeta (b. 1940) also treats the subject of Pinochet's dictatorship in his works. In *The Insurrection* (1982), a village of misfits challenges an oppressive dictatorship. Skármeta's novel *Burning Patience* (1987) tells the story of an exiled Pablo Neruda and the relationship between the poet and his mail carrier. The novel later became the acclaimed Italian film *Il Postino* (1994).

Jorge Edwards (b. 1931) was the recipient of the 2000 Cervantes Award. The prize honors lifetime achievement in Spanish-language literature. His many books include *Persona Non Grata* (1982), detailing his career as a Chilean diplomat to Cuba before being kicked out by Cuban dictator Fidel Castro (b. 1926). He used his experiences to draw parallels between the Cuban revolution and Chile under Pinochet.

# Music

Long before Europeans brought guitars and hymns to South America, the indigenous peoples of Chile developed their own unique musical traditions. Their music accompanied rituals or served as entertainment. Ensembles often consisted of wind instruments such as flutes or pipes, drums, and stringed instruments.

Several types of rhythm instruments can be heard in Andean music. The bombo is a ceremonial drum made from a hollowed-out tree trunk. The southern Mapuche play the kultrún, a type of kettledrum made of wood or bone. Musicians might shake a *palo de iluvia,* or rain stick, to produce a constant sound resembling that of falling rain.

Wind instruments of many shapes and sizes emit a variety of pitches and timbres. The tiny *queña,* a flute made of a single reed, produces a high, lilting sound. *Trutrukas,* longer horns made of bamboo, produce low notes to accompany steady drumming. The *zampoña* is a type of panpipe made of reeds of varying length tied together by woolen string. Zampoña

Vincente Huidobro (1893–1948) was a prominent post–World War I literary figure in both Europe and Chile. He referred to himself as the father of Creationism, the avant-garde movement. Writers in this literary style created striking images by using seemingly irrational and random words and letters, as seen in his poem "Capilla Aldeana."

# The Cueca

Forget about ballroom dances and crowded discos while in Chile! One of Chile's proudest traditions is the *cueca*, the national dance. Chileans throughout the country all know the steps of the dance, which was originally associated with rural society. Partners dance around each other without touching, waving handkerchiefs in a stylized imitation of a rooster courting a hen. The

huasos, or Chilean cowboys, are the masters of the cueca and dance in full rodeo garb, complete with spurs, cowboy hats, and ponchos. A band playing traditional tunes sets either a fast or slow pace for the couples, depending on regional variations. The audience sings along and shouts encouragement to the more bashful dancers. Every patriotic Chilean enjoys dancing the cueca during Independence Day celebrations or at the rodeo.

players must move their mouths from reed to reed quickly in order to create the range of pitches necessary for many Andean songs.

Stringed instruments from Europe also fit into Andean styles. The guitar and violin are the most common. They usually accompany the *charango*, a small ukulele-type instrument made from an armadillo shell.

Chilean folk music was largely disregarded until the 1950s and early 1960s, when musicians began reviving old songs. The Nueva Canción Chilena, or New Song Movement, used traditional instruments and arrangements to speak out in song against social injustice and inequality. Violeta Parra (1917–1967), the sister of poet Nicanor Parra, was the most recognized face and voice of the New Song Movement. She had

A photograph of renowned Chilean writer José Donoso dates from 1957. Donoso was one of the leading writers of the Latin American literary boom that began in the 1960s. He is known for combining satire with surrealism, using a variety of myths, legends, and bizarre happenings to tell his story. During the term of General Pinochet, Donoso established himself as a critic of the regime through his writing.

become internationally known by the time she committed suicide in 1967. Seven years later, American folk singer Joan Baez (b. 1941) recorded a version of her "Thanks to Life." The recording introduced an even wider audience to the tragic Chilean star.

Victor Jara (d. 1973) often played guitar for Violeta Parra, eventually becoming a celebrity in his own right. His songs, such as "Public Prayer to a Laborer" became rallying cries for the Chilean working classes. When the military coup began in 1973, Victor Jara refused to go into hiding. He chose to stand and be captured alongside other supporters of the Allende government. He endured many hours of torture at the hands of Pinochet's forces and died of his injuries. Chileans say that he kept singing right up to the time of his demise.

Other members of the New Song Movement fled Chile before they could meet a similar fate. Payo Grondona (b. 1945) was one of the movement's most prolific songwriters, writing hit songs "The Little Devil" and "Unpublished Subject." The best-known bands to emerge from the New Song Movement are Quilapayun and Inti-Illimani. Formed in the 1960s and exiled in Europe during the coup, both groups still make music using traditional Andean instruments. Chile's rock scene has boomed since the dictatorship ended. Bands like La Ley and Lucybell have attracted international audiences with their challenging yet catchy tunes.

Though most of the music heard in Chile today either draws upon folk tradition or international pop standards, a small classical music community exists. Classical music emerged as a publicly funded institution in Chile in 1926. That year, violinist Armando Carvajal Quiroz founded the Orquesta Sinfónica de Santiago (City Symphonic Orchestra of Santiago). Although his project endured for only a couple years, it brought public attention to Chile's lack of a classical orchestra.

Violeta Parra was Chile's best known folk singer. She began the "new music" movement, which incorporated the different kinds of folk and traditional music in Chile. Today Angel and Isabel Parra carry on their mother's legacy.

The Universidad de Chile donated funds to help the Ministerio de Educacíon establish the Associacion Nacional de Conciertos (National Association of Concerts) in 1930. This grant resulted in the founding of the Orquesta Sinfónica de Chile (Symphonic Orchestra of Chile). The orchestra's growing popularity led it to establish the Festivales Bienales de Musica Chilena (Biannual Chilean Music Festival) in 1948. The festival offers Chilean musicians and composers a chance to showcase their talents. The first Semanas Musicales de Frutillar (Frutillar Musical Week) took place in 1981 and now attracts crowds from around the world. Today, the Symphonic Orchestra of Chile plays more than fifty dates a year and sponsors youth orchestras throughout the country.

Several famous performers and composers have emerged from Chile's musical community. Domingo Santa Cruz (1899–1987) wrote chamber works and symphonies reflecting his life's experiences—pieces that greatly influenced the art of composition in Latin America. Alfonso Letelier (b. 1912), who writes mainly for the

female voice, is particularly active in Chile's opera world. The best-known classical Chilean musician was the pianist Claudio Arrau (1903–1991), recognized worldwide for his mastery of the romantic repertoire. He left Chile at the age of eight to study piano in Berlin under the tutelage of Martin Krause. Arrau made his American debut in 1923. The young pianist took first prize at the 1927 International Pianists' Competition in Geneva, Switzerland. He remained one of classical music's foremost pianists throughout his career.

Renowned throughout the world, Chilean pianist Claudio Arrau began as a child prodigy. His mother was an amateur pianist, and his father was an eye doctor. After the death of Arrau's father when he was one year old, his mother supported the family by teaching piano. As a child, Arrau sat in on these lessons, and the result was that he could read music before he could read words. By the age of fifteen and after the death of his teacher, Arrau preferred to continue his studies on his own. He won the prestigious Liszt Prize twice in a row, at ages sixteen and seventeen.

# FAMOUS FOODS AND RECIPES OF CHILE

## 9

Chilean cuisine takes advantage of all the riches offered by the land and sea. National dishes draw upon Mapuche traditions, based on the foods and flavors native to Chile, but they also reflect European influences. Everyday cooking is rich and filling, often containing potatoes, rice, beans, and corn. Depending on one's household budget, main dishes include meat, fish, or eggs.

Fields and orchards produce a splendid array of fruits and vegetables. Ranchers raise cattle in the Central Valley and sheep in the south, and fishermen bring in boats loaded with fish and shellfish.

Americans often hold the misconception that all Latin American food is painfully spicy. In reality, many Chilean dishes are subtly flavored. "Chili" did not originate in Chile, where condiments and side dishes are more likely to add fire to the meal. These use the ají chili pepper native to Chile.

The day begins with *desayuno*, or breakfast. Usually mothers rise early to prepare the meal. Typically it consists of toast with jam, sometimes accompanied by eggs. Adults have café con leche, a sweetened mixture of milk and coffee. *Almuerzo*, the main meal of the day, takes place in the early afternoon. Pastries or sandwiches are served at 5 PM for a teatime called *once*. Literally

A woman picks grapes *(left)* to be crushed for the production of wine at the Cousino Macul Winery. Chile's vineyards are known for their healthy fruit and disease-free vines, largely because of protection by the natural barriers of the Andes and the Pacific Ocean. Chile is the only country that has pure, ungrafted European vines, which means that many grapevines are very old. In the photograph above, pelicans surround a fishing boat. The fishing industry in Chile is very lucrative. Chile is third in the world for total fish caught, trailing behind Peru and China. Popular fish caught by Chilean fishermen are anchovies, shrimp, and salmon. The salmon catch in Chile has risen to nearly 80,000 tons since 1986.

A group of women prepares Chilean *curanto*, a spicy seafood stew. Also known as *curanto en olla*, this dish is made of clams, smoked fish, mussels, and potatoes. Traditional to Chiloé and Easter Island, the stew is cooked for hours in a pit filled with hot stones. The ingredients are placed over the stones, layered between large leaves, and covered with sacks and earth. The seafood stew is served with a topping of fresh and spicy tomato salsa. The dish has a delicious smoky taste.

meaning "eleven," it is a variation on the English custom of taking tea in the afternoon. Families gather again for a small meal, *la comida*, between 8 and 10 PM.

Chileans enjoy long, leisurely mealtimes. In the home, women do the cooking, although men will take the helm for summer *asados*, or cookouts. These are grand occasions, a chance for family and friends to gather together for the day. Everyone indulges in huge quantities of meat grilled over an open flame.

## National Favorites

Empanadas, large turnovers, are the favorite national food, essential to every picnic or patriotic holiday. They can contain any filling, savory or sweet, and are either baked or fried. One popular variety is *empanadas de pino*, stuffed with beef, onion, spices, hard-boiled eggs, raisins, and olives. *Empanadas de queso* (cheese filled) are also common.

Pastel de choclo is a popular Chilean entrée. It is a corn and meat pie made with egg and vegetable and topped with sugar.

Many dishes include *choclo*, or corn, native to South America. *Pastel de choclo*, a baked casserole, has a meat layer covered by creamed corn. *Humitas* are small packets of corn wrapped in their husks and then steamed. A thick bean and corn stew called *porotos granados*, thickened by pumpkin, makes a delicious summer meal. *Cazuela*, another national favorite, is a colorful soup of potato, pumpkin, green beans, sweet corn, and chicken.

The islanders of Chiloé prepare curanto in a traditional manner that can take an entire day. First, they dig a large pit, fill it with rocks, and build a fire on top to heat the rocks. After a few hours, they remove the ashes and coals. Everyone piles on meat, vegetables, potatoes, and shellfish, including lots of clams. Layers of cabbage leaves or seaweed separate each ingredient. The mound, topped with burlap and leaves to keep the steam from escaping, cooks for hours. It yields a substantial and delicious meal for a crowd!

Seafood is eaten in soups and entrées or as a dish by itself. *Cebiche* is a dish of raw fish marinated in lime juice and spices. Most Chileans enjoy beef, especially *bistec a lo pobre*. This "poor man's steak" is smothered with two fried eggs, french fries, and fried onions. Meals are accompanied by Chile's famous wine; children drink fruit juice or soda. Herb teas are popular, and later in the day, Chileans may switch to the renowned pisco, a strong grape

Grapes are harvested in the fall when they are fully ripe; they are then crushed using a special machine instead of using the feet as in the old days. After the grapes are crushed, the juice is fermented in large stainless-steel tanks or vats, where it will remain for upwards of ten weeks.

# Ensalada Chilena

**Ingredients:**

1 medium onion, finely chopped (the sweet vidalia onion is best)

3 large tomatoes, chopped

1 jalapeño chili pepper, seeded and finely diced

1 teaspoon each salt and pepper

3 tablespoons olive oil

1 tablespoon lemon juice, or to taste

¼ cup coarsely chopped cilantro leaves

**Procedure:**

Soak the chopped onion in cold water for ten minutes while preparing the other ingredients. Rinse and drain well in a colander. Mix tomatoes, onions, and jalapeño on a large platter. Season with salt and pepper and drizzle with oil and lemon juice. Toss well. Sprinkle with cilantro. Serves four.

# Flan

Flan is a favorite dessert in Latin American countries as well as in Spain.

**Ingredients:**

⅓ cup sugar

2 tablespoons water

2 eggs

1 14-ounce can sweetened condensed milk

½ cup milk

1 teaspoon vanilla

**Procedure:**

Preheat oven to 325 °F.

In a small pan, boil sugar and water over medium heat until thick and golden, about 5 to 8 minutes. Immediately pour into four ovenproof custard cups or an 8-inch square pan and tilt to coat the sides and the bottom. Use oven mitts and be careful, because this is very hot!

Beat eggs with a whisk in a small mixing bowl, and mix in condensed milk, regular milk, and vanilla. Pour batter into custard cups or baking dish.

Place cups or dish in a large pan on the oven rack. Pour water into this pan until it reaches one inch up the outside edge of the cups or baking dish.

Bake for 55 minutes. Chill. Invert flan onto a plate when ready to serve. Serves four.

brandy. Dessert can be simply a piece of fruit, fresh or dried, or an elaborate *torta* (cake) to satisfy the Chilean sweet tooth. Many desserts are filled with *manjar*, a thick, super-sweet caramel. A baked custard called flan is also a favorite.

Fast-food restaurants, both Chilean and foreign-owned, have gained popularity in recent years. Customers may ask for a *completo*, a hot dog with everything—mayo, avocado, sauerkraut, and tomato. International options are becoming more common in cities. German cuisine has had a following since the 1900s as a result of German settlements in Chile.

Americans are surprised when they find that most Chilean salads do not include lettuce. Chileans are equally surprised by creamy salad dressings featured on the typical American side salad. Feel free to adjust the amounts of ingredients in the popular *ensalada chilena* recipe (on page 94) to your own taste!

Chileans have a strong sense of family. Young people in Chile usually live at home until they marry. Chileans start dating in their mid-teens and have long engagements that precede marriage. Weddings in Chile are simple and small, and are normally held at home. Men age nineteen are required to serve in the military for two years, and women of the same age have the option of volunteering for military service.

# DAILY LIFE AND CUSTOMS IN CHILE

## 10

I n the far north, the Aymara people herd llamas and alpacas in the highlands. Among the southern reaches of Chilean Patagonia, isolated families listen to the radio for the latest gossip of their far-flung communities. Most Chileans live between these extremes in the temperate central region, and 87 percent live in cities. Despite geographic distances and vast differences in lifestyle and opportunity, Chileans see themselves as a unified society.

One value shared by most Chileans is a dedication to the family. From rural farmers to cosmopolitan Santiago residents, Chileans consider family their first priority. Chile has a very low rate of homelessness because most people turn to relatives during hard times. Hierarchy in Mapuche society traditionally depended on family bonds.

Many Chileans, especially girls, stay at home until they are married and live with their parents while studying at a university or entering the workforce. They tend to marry in their twenties and have children soon after marriage. Most participate in both a brief civil ceremony, required by law, and a formal church wedding. Divorce is illegal, as is abortion, largely due to the opposition of the strong Catholic Church. While Chileans may claim that marriage is permanent under

More than five million people, almost one-third of Chile's population, live in cosmopolitan Santiago *(left)*. On Easter Island *(above)* a father teaches a traditional craft to his son. The population of Easter Island is growing, but the Rapa Nui people continue to live in the only town on the island, Hanga Roa.

An illustration from Frezier's *Voyage to the South Seas Between 1712–1714* depicts a Chilean man preparing to hit a ball during a game of *el sueca*, an early form of golf.

Chilean law, in reality, many couples seek civil annulments.

The average family has two children. Parents love kids and tend to indulge them. Many well-off households employ *nanas*, or nannies, who take a personal interest in raising the children. Poorer Chileans turn to relatives and friends to help look after their children.

Chileans are more reserved than some other Latin Americans, dressing conservatively and generally avoiding rowdy behavior. Still, they are very sociable and welcoming to outsiders. Foreigners may be offered an invitation to dine with a fairly new acquaintance. Don't forget, as in many Hispanic countries, it is polite to arrive about twenty minutes late! Women greet each other with a kiss on the cheek, men with a handshake or a hug. Conversational topics usually avoided by Americans, because of political correctness or concern for personal feelings, are fair game for the candid Chilean people.

Chileans show little prejudice against minorities. In their ethnically homogenous country, however, this goodwill has not been tested. Most express a dual view of their indigenous heritage. Although they are proud of Chile's rich native traditions, they often speak critically of the "indios," or indigenous peoples, many of whom live in poverty. Homosexuality is tolerated, but not widely accepted.

Chileans are also still coming to terms with the legacy of Pinochet's regime. More than a third of the population is under the age of twenty. This generation grew up as the country moved out of a period now associated with repression of individual freedom and an absence of representative democracy. They are still dealing with the fallout of recent persecution. The Pinochet regime committed brutal human

rights violations. Many of the perpetrators were granted amnesty before Pinochet left office. Some of the most wrenching stories are those of the "disappeared," numbering more than 1,000, who have never been accounted for by the government.

## Home Life and Leisure Time

When the children come home from school, they might start their homework. Or, on second thought, they probably wouldn't have much trouble convincing a few friends and relatives to join them for a backyard soccer game. As in many countries across the world, Chile is obsessed with soccer. Stadiums fill up an hour and a half before games begin, with fans dressed in team colors. Each city or town has its own team. These range from local clubs to professional teams who reach the national championships. One of the Santiago teams, Colo Colo, took its name from the hero of Alonso de Ercilla y Zúñiga's famous poem, "La Araucana."

A teacher poses with her elementary class *(above)*. In Chile, teachers receive a very small salary, making it difficult for them to meet the financial needs of their families. Many teachers resort to teaching at two or more schools and teach well into the night to supplement their incomes. Chilean soccer player Gonzalo Fierro fights for the ball before Colombian player Fabián López Montoya can steal it *(below)*. The players compete during the South American Futbol Championships.

# Chilean Cowboys

The huasos are part of Chile's proud national heritage. They wear a traditional costume of a bold poncho, broad-brimmed felt or straw hat, and leather boots with huge gleaming spurs, but their reputation lies in their skill on horseback. Through centuries of working with horses, the huasos became superb horsemen. Their well-trained steeds can perform many impressive stunts, both useful and flashy. In a move called *la sentada*, the horse will come to an instant halt at one word from the huaso. Two huasos on horseback may engage in *juego de cañas*, jousting with canes, or *tiro al gallo*, a tug-of-war contest. The crucial test of skill comes each year at the rodeo. The season begins on Fiestas Patrias (Independence Day) and eliminates competitors until the national championships. After a few dramatic individual exercises, pairs of huasos proceed to the main event: pinning a young bull against the padded sides of the arena. Chileans cheer them on while munching on empanadas and enjoying music and festivities.

Chileans take advantage of their long coastline and enjoy water sports and hanging out at the beach. Those who can afford it play tennis and golf, go horseback riding and race horses, and spend weekends at Andean ski resorts. Malls and trendy shops have multiplied in the present healthy economy. But average Chileans are more likely to be found in open-air markets called *ferias*. In households without electricity or a refrigerator, the mother attends to daily marketing in addition to her other tasks.

Television is a constant companion in many homes. *Telenovelas*, similar to soap operas, enjoy huge popularity. Most books have to be imported from other Spanish-speaking countries. Chile has a long tradition of a strong independent press. Its earliest newspaper, the resistance broadsheet *La Aurora*, dates from 1812. Today, the two major newspapers are *El Mercurio* and *La Nación*. The German community still subscribes to the weekly *El Cóndor*, which has been in print since 1938. Readers preferring lighter fare might enjoy the comic book *Condorito*, distributed across the Spanish-speaking world.

Viña del Mar, known as Garden City and one of Chile's most modern cities, is the most famous beach resort in the country. Chile's 2,580-mile-long coastline makes outings to the beach very popular, especially in the central region, where the climate is the most temperate.

# EDUCATION AND WORK IN CHILE

## 11

Like most children around the world, young Chileans attend school most weekdays. In preparation, they sit down to a quick breakfast with their family and double-check that they have finished any homework for math, history, and maybe even computer classes.

In centuries past, a majority of Chileans never learned to read. Children of colonial hacienda workers grew up to work in the fields just like their parents and grandparents. Miners' sons followed their fathers into the nitrate or copper mines. The educational system improved during the nineteenth century, working from 1812 onward to provide primary education to all children. Today, Chile has a 95 percent literacy rate, one of the highest in South America. Young Chileans have more career opportunities open to them than ever before.

## Education

The Chilean school year runs from March through December, with a summer vacation in January and February and a two-week winter break in July. Many schoolchildren attend school for only half a day. Proposed school reforms aim to lengthen the amount of time students spend in

Raising sheep in Chile is a major industry, especially in the wet southern region *(left)*. Currently, farmers are looking for more ways to modernize and expand the agriculture market. They are concerned with the issues of increasing international commerce, improving competitiveness, conserving resources, and preventing contamination of land and water. Commuters board a bus in Santiago *(above)*. Most Chileans work in the service sector, which includes health care, teaching, government, and home care. The second largest group works in banking, real estate, and insurance services. In recent years, more women have entered the workforce. They now make up about a third of the workers.

In a class about contemporary Chilean history, students listen to a lecture about General Pinochet's rise to power in 1973. Many Chilean history books devote only a few paragraphs to what they call Pinochet's "military intervention," but they mention the more than one thousand people who died or disappeared during the dictatorship between 1973 and 1990.

school. Days are currently divided into two sessions. Elementary school students attend from 8:15 AM until 1:15 PM. Older students begin classes after lunch at 1:30 PM and leave at 6:30 PM. School subjects, similar to those of U.S. schools, include Spanish, reading, math, science, geography, history, music, art, and athletics. Between periods, children spend recess time in many of the same activities that American students enjoy, such as playing games and jumping rope. Unlike many American schoolchildren, Chilean students wear school uniforms. Girls dress in dark jumpers and white shirts, while boys wear dark jackets and slacks with a white shirt.

Most children, about 70 percent, receive a public education. The quality of public schools varies as a result of uneven funding from one region to another. Rural and poorer areas have fewer

Currently, "prebasic" instruction for three- to five-year-olds is free, but attendance is not mandatory. Many Chilean educators feel it should be required since only 30 percent of students are attending. At the basic level for children ages six to fourteen, attendance is much improved, with 95 percent attending.

educational resources and offer lower teacher salaries. Despite the law, some children do not finish primary school. Poorer families may not be able to afford school supplies or may need children to help with farmwork, earn extra money, or baby-sit for siblings.

A small number of Chilean kids attend partially subsidized or private schools. Privately educated students usually receive higher test scores. Some parents believe private schools will give their children a better education. Others are attracted to a particular program or school structure, such as religious schools or single-gender schools. Chile has a few foreign language schools, where most of the instruction is in French, German, English, or whatever language the school emphasizes. Often, most of the students in these schools are Chilean.

Chilean schools are divided into four levels: preschool, elementary, secondary, and university. Only about a third of children eligible for preschool actually attend. All students must complete eight years of primary schooling from age six to fourteen.

Many Chilean public schools tend to be poorly funded and have class sizes in excess of forty students. However, 65 percent of students ages fourteen to sixteen continue to the "media" level. Of that number, 20 percent take the required examination to go on to university studies. A major challenge facing university students is the cost of tuition, which must be paid up front and in cash. The Chilean government does not allow student loans.

Primary school attendance became compulsory in 1920, but the government could not enforce the policy until the middle of the century.

About 60 percent of all students opt to continue their education and go on to a non-compulsory secondary school similar to high school in the United States. They can choose from a variety of programs. Technical and professional programs train students for specific jobs in the workforce and can last from four to seven years. Humanities and science courses prepare students for the university. After they finish their secondary studies, students take a test similar to the SAT in order to apply to universities and other higher-education programs. University graduates receive degrees or licenses that allow them to practice a specific profession. These diplomas are quite different from degrees awarded by U.S. schools, which qualify graduates for a variety of careers.

Chile's universities are known as some of the best in South America. For many years, Chile had eight universities, two public and six private. These did not charge tuition. The Universidad de Chile, centered in Santiago, was founded in 1842.

When Pinochet took power, he fired nearly a third of the professors and expelled many students. He limited majors to traditional fields and eliminated "subversive" programs such as political science, psychology, and the arts. Funding to higher education fell substantially, since authorities diverted money to primary and secondary schools. New enrollment fees and cuts in financial aid excluded the poor from higher education. The military split the universities into specialized colleges. It supported the growth of technical and private schools, many of dubious academic quality.

Since the return of democracy, universities have received more funding.

A military parade in Arica, near the Peru border. In Chile the armed forces are subordinate to the president but have a large degree of legal autonomy. However, since the reinstatement of a civilian government in the 1990s, the president has had little control over the military. The branches of the military include the army, navy, air force, Chilean *carabineros* (national police), and investigations police.

A copper refinery worker in protective gear opens a furnace door. Chile's mineral resources constitute most of the country's exports with copper alone accounting for 40 percent.

Ongoing educational reform programs address the structure and quality of higher education. The government established grants and loans for low-income students and encouraged Chileans to take advantage of adult education programs. Matriculation in higher education programs has soared since the 1990s. Graduates of secondary schools face stiff competition for spots in the top universities.

## Work

Many Chileans work in occupations related to Chile's natural resources, such as mining, forestry, fishing, and agriculture. Nearly a quarter of all Chileans work in industry. Some of the largest corporations produce machinery, transport equipment, and chemicals. The majority of the population holds jobs in the service sector, which has boomed during years of economic growth. Chile's unemployment rate fluctuates between 8 and 10 percent. It is especially high among younger Chileans.

In the far north, copper mining employs only a small percentage of Chileans, but copper revenues are the backbone of the

This worker in an alpaca textile mill in La Ligua checks the wool as it comes off of a carding machine. An alpaca mill is where high-quality long-staple hair is made into yarn. Wool is another major export of Chile.

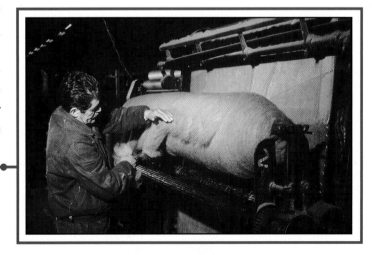

This is an aerial view of an opencast copper mine in Chile. Chile has the world's largest deposits of copper, making it the world's largest producer and exporter of this material. Increased demand for Chilean copper during World War II stimulated the country's economic growth. Since that time, copper has become the cornerstone of Chile's economy.

economy. For seventeen hours a day, huge trucks barrel out of Chuquicamata, the world's largest opencast copper mine.

Miners in the north organized the first trade unions. They demanded that the government address Chile's social and economic inequalities. In 1907, the military brutally repressed a strike in the northern town of Iquique, gunning down hundreds of people.

Before the copper mines, northern nitrate companies exported fertilizer across the world. The industry flopped in 1915 when the Germans discovered how to synthesize artificial nitrates.

Most of Chile's cropland lies in the fertile Central Valley. Commercial agriculturists as well as small farmers plant wheat, oats, beans, lentils, maize, and other subsistence crops. Markets in the Northern Hemisphere welcome high-quality exports of fruits and vegetables during their winter months, Chile's prime growing season. In recent years, grape producers have focused on expanding and improving the wine industry. Chile is the third largest exporter of wine to the United States,

# John North, Nitrate King

In the late nineteenth century, one of the most powerful economic forces in the country was an English mechanic turned nitrate entrepreneur. John North, the Nitrate King, cleverly bought up nearly worthless bonds for nitrate holdings from Peru, which Chile conquered during the War of the Pacific. After the war ended in 1883, Chile decided to respect the owners' rights to its newly acquired territory. North became owner of some of the most valuable nitrate deposits in the north. He went on to acquire related industries such as railroads and the water company. Along with a handful of others, he became a virtual ruler of his domain.

In 1886, presidential candidate José Manuel Balmaceda proposed nationalized railways and a nitrate tax, which would fund public-works programs. John North spent the huge sum of $150,000 in an attempt to defeat him. Despite his efforts, Balmaceda took office later that year. Conflict between the president and the ruling classes, including the church, congress, and industry, led to a civil war. Congress raised an army from nitrate and port workers and miners. These forces headed south to defeat Balmaceda's National Army. Balmaceda committed suicide, but in an odd twist of fate, the nitrate industry failed in the 1890s. John North died in 1896, from a seizure during a board meeting of a nitrate company.

behind France and Italy. Chilean ranchers pasture sheep and cattle on much of the clear land that is unsuitable for farming, especially the Patagonian plains.

The forestry industry prospers because of huge tracts of quickly growing woodlands. These are harvested for production of paper products and timber. Environmentalists worry about the devastation of old-growth forests and destruction of habitat for native species.

On the coast, fishermen bring in eels, swordfish, bass, sole, shellfish, and other ocean fish. Much of the catch is turned into products such as fish meal and oil. Fish farming is a growing industry. Chile exports more salmon than any other country besides Norway, and many are farm-grown.

Grape pickers return from the vineyards at the end of the day. In Chile the amount of land dedicated to vineyards and grapevines is greater than the entire area occupied by all other fruit trees together.

The Mapuche traditionally live off of the land. Today, most farm on the state-established *reducciones*. Many of the Mapuche live in poverty and have been forced to sell their property and take jobs in the city.

More than 60 percent of the workforce has jobs in the service sector. Occupations range from the hotel and restaurant business to finance, retail, tourism, and health care. The Chileans are conscientious and friendly. Even so, workers remain conscious of social class differences, earning them the nickname "the English of South America."

Chile's military, made up of the army, navy, air force, and national police, is large for a small nation. All men between the ages of eighteen and forty-five must register for service. Some are actually drafted. Every year, about 30,000 men, usually at the age of eighteen or nineteen, are called to service. They complete a year in the army or air force, or two years in the navy.

Throughout much of the twentieth century, labor unions, clamoring for workers' rights, brought attention to social issues. Pinochet banned unions when he came into

Chilean actress Leonor Varela poses for a photograph. The Chilean government provides many benefits for women who work outside of the home. In 1990, the National Women's Service (Sernam) was established to ensure equal rights for women, to improve their quality of life, to bring them into the workforce, and to strengthen family ties.

power. He reversed much of the progress made by labor organizations. Since the return to democracy, legislation has established a minimum wage, paid vacations, and other workers' rights. Trade unions have once again been legalized.

## Women in Chile

About one-third of the women work outside of their homes. Many choose jobs in teaching and office work, but a growing proportion are entering professions that have been dominated by men. Women are choosing to become *médicas* (doctors), *abogadas* (lawyers), *arquitectas* (architects), and *ingenieras* (engineers). However, they tend to earn less than men, and a greater number live in poverty. Many women are homemakers, considering a career secondary to family. Some women, especially among the Mapuche, supplement their household incomes by making traditional wares and ornaments that they sell at markets.

The Universidad de Chile began to admit women in 1860, only twenty years after it was founded. Today, men and women have equal opportunities in education. There is no significant difference in the average number of years men and women spend in school.

Women won the right to vote in 1949. They played a substantial role in grassroots movements before and during the Pinochet regime. Since the return to democracy, relatively few women have held important positions in the national government. This is slowly changing. Ricardo Lagos Escobar, elected president of the Republic of Chile in 2000, included women in his cabinet, and a number of congresswomen serve in the legislature.

# CHILE
## AT A GLANCE

## HISTORY

After the Republic of Chile first declared its independence from Spain in 1810, Spain staged a reconquest of Chile in 1814. A Chilean-Argentine army crossed over the Andes into Chile in 1817, defeating the Spanish. Chile officially gained its independence the following year. The new nation enacted its first constitution in 1822, abolishing slavery in 1823. Political instability lasted until 1830, when Diego Portales's authoritative government ushered in an era of constitutional rule.

From 1836 to 1839, Chile fought against a Peruvian-Bolivian confederation, fearing it would lose its independence. The war ended with the separation of Peru and Bolivia.

Chile entered the War of the Pacific against Bolivia and Peru in 1879 over ownership rights to valuable nitrate fields. Emerging the winner in 1884, Chile's territorial gains included vast mineral wealth. Its size increased by a third. Chile fell into a short but bloody civil war in 1891, battling about presidential powers. Later that year, a new constitution established a parliamentary government with a strong congress.

Relative peace reigned, even as the market for nitrates bottomed out during World War I. A new constitution in 1925 reinstated the executive branch as the head of government, established a bicameral Congress, and granted suffrage to all men eighteen and over. Economic and political turmoil was stabilized by the reelection of Arturo Alessandri in 1932.

Women gained the right to vote in 1949. In 1964, they influenced the election of Christian Democratic leader Eduardo Frei Montalva, whose centrist policies satisfied neither the privileged elite nor reformers seeking better lives for the poor. The 1970 election became highly charged as the country faced economic, political, and social unrest. The reform-minded Popular Unity candidate, Salvador Allende, was elected by a small majority and was approved by Congress. His radical agenda was opposed by conservative groups and by President Richard

M. Nixon's administration in the United States. A bloody military coup took place on September 11, 1973. President Allende and thousands of other Chileans died in the violence. Many Chileans expected a quick return to democracy. Instead, General Augusto Pinochet ruled the nation as a dictator until 1989. During his regime, he revived the economy but sanctioned many human-rights violations, denying Chile's people many basic democratic rights.

Free elections were held in 1989. Chileans voted for the ouster of Pinochet in favor of Christian Democrat Patricio Aylwin. The transition was peaceful. Pinochet remained in command of the military until 1998, when he was arrested by British authorities. Spain charged that human-rights violations had been committed against its citizens during his reign. Courts judged Pinochet mentally and physically unfit to face the charges. He returned to Chile in 2000. In July of 2002, Chile's Supreme Court also declared him unfit for trial.

## ECONOMY

Chile has one of the most successful economies in Latin America. Fluctuations during much of the century steadied out to a period of gross domestic product (GDP) growth with low inflation during the 1990s. Once dependent on copper production, Chile now has a variety of high-quality exports.

Chile's economy plummeted during Salvador Allende's brief presidency from 1970 to 1973. He aimed to nationalize agriculture, banks, and many industries, and he tried to implement constitutional changes. His political opponents, especially the wealthy ruling classes and the military, worked to sabotage his programs. The United States provided money and tactical support for Allende's opponents. In the ensuing crisis, productivity dropped, inflation soared, and international investors fled the country. Many consumers turned to the black market for food and basic goods.

After taking power, Augusto Pinochet repealed most of Allende's reforms. The government instituted the policies of the "Chicago Boys," economists educated at the University of Chicago. On their advice, Pinochet reduced tariffs, cut government regulations and price controls, and privatized many state operations. Unions were outlawed, and workers were stripped of rights to bargain for better wages or working conditions. The economy rebounded, largely from a trial-and-error process. These policies sank the country into a recession in 1983. Critics of

Pinochet's model claim that although the economy grew, the elite reaped most of the benefits while the poor fell further into poverty.

The government has maintained most of Pinochet's policies since the return to democracy. Unemployment levels, which soared in the 1970s and 1980s, now stand at about 9 percent. The rate of poverty is about 23 percent. Recent administrations have addressed the huge gap between the rich and poor with social reforms and educational programs. The minimum wage is approximately $206 U.S. dollars per month. Per capita GDP is $4,800 per household. (In the United States, per capita GDP is $36,200.) During the 1980s, Pinochet's regime privatized social security. Individuals pay into a private pension fund, which is then invested in the Chilean economy.

Chile owes much of its success today to exports, accounting for almost a quarter of its GDP. Important economic sectors include mining, agriculture and wine production, forestry, fishing, and tourism.

Chile is the world's second-largest copper producer. Mining contributes about 40 percent of export earnings, equal to about 11 percent of the country's total GDP. Besides copper, Chile produces smaller amounts of gold, silver, iron ore, nitrates, molybdenum, manganese, lead, and coal. Agriculture, forestry, and fishing employ about 15 percent of the population. Much of the fertile land is devoted to subsistence crops such as grains and legumes, but Chile also exports a variety of fruits, vegetables, and wine. Forested regions are harvested for sawlogs, pulp, and other wood products. Chile is the largest exporter of fish meal in the world and the second largest of salmon. Industry accounts for 23 percent of the labor force, and 62 percent work in the service sector. Tourists have begun contributing significantly to the economy, making up 4 percent of the GDP.

# GOVERNMENT AND POLITICS

The current government structure is the result of events that began in the 1970s when Salvador Allende became president. Receiving 36 percent of the vote, he represented a coalition of left-wing parties, including communists, socialists, and others. Conservative forces, including Congress, the Catholic Church, wealthy landowners, business, and the military, opposed his objectives. In this political climate, there was no hope of compromise. Amid the ensuing social and economic chaos, General Augusto Pinochet staged a military coup in 1973, establishing himself as dictator. In 1980, he submitted a constitution to voters, which they approved by a majority.

This constitution, with a few amendments, is still in place today. Chile returned to a democratic system in 1989. A constitutional amendment diminished the role of the National Security Council. Its members now include the president, presidents of the Supreme Court and Senate, and the heads of armed forces and police. A coalition of parties opposed to Pinochet called the Concertación para la Democracia, supported the Christian Democrat candidate Patricio Aylwin. He easily defeated his opponents.

The president acts as both chief of state and head of the government. A cabinet made up of ministers appointed by the president directs executive decisions and implementation. Presidential elections are held every six years; incumbents may not run for successive reelection. Congress, the legislative branch of the government, consists of a Senate and the Chamber of Deputies. Thirty-eight senators are elected, eight appointed. They hold office for eight years with staggered terms. Past presidents become senators for life, although Pinochet's privileges are currently suspended. One hundred and twenty deputies are popularly elected to four-year terms.

Chile's highest court is the seventeen-member Chilean Supreme Court. When a position opens up, the Court presents a list of five possible replacement candidates to the president, who chooses an individual and sends the nomination to Congress for ratification. Chile also has sixteen appellate courts, a number of local and specialized courts, and an independent military justice system. An independent constitutional tribunal dictates the last word on constitutional issues.

While Chile's government has been highly centralized, in recent years, the government has begun to shift some powers to regional and local authorities. Chile consists of thirteen regions, headed by intendants appointed by the president. These are divided into provinces, administered by appointed governors. Voters elect local mayors and councils that support the governors and intendants.

Candidates of the Concertación para la Democracia coalition have won the last three presidential elections. Individual parties lean toward the left (Socialist Party, Party for Democracy), right (National Renewal Party, Independent Democratic Union), or center (Christian Democrats, Radical Social Democrats). The Concertación has dominated congressional elections as well. The Christian Democrats, part of the Concertación, presently hold the largest representation of any single party. The socialist Ricardo Lagos was elected president in 2000.

# TIMELINE

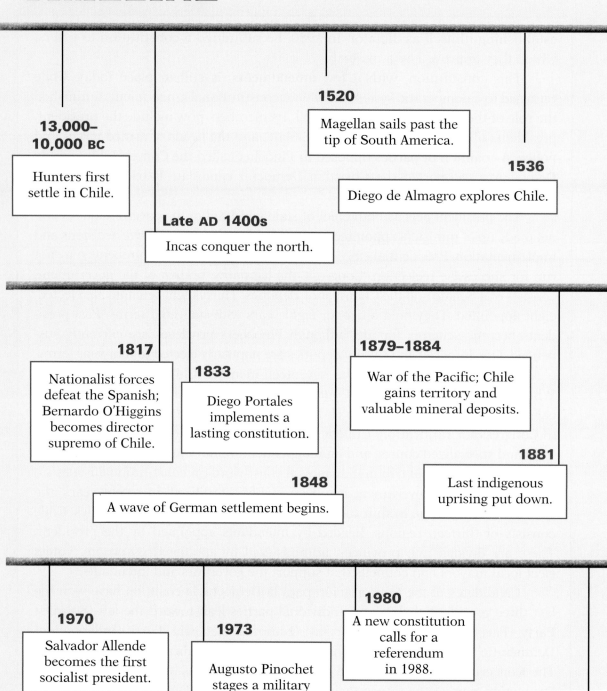

**13,000–10,000 BC**
Hunters first settle in Chile.

**Late AD 1400s**
Incas conquer the north.

**1520**
Magellan sails past the tip of South America.

**1536**
Diego de Almagro explores Chile.

**1817**
Nationalist forces defeat the Spanish; Bernardo O'Higgins becomes director supremo of Chile.

**1833**
Diego Portales implements a lasting constitution.

**1848**
A wave of German settlement begins.

**1879–1884**
War of the Pacific; Chile gains territory and valuable mineral deposits.

**1881**
Last indigenous uprising put down.

**1970**
Salvador Allende becomes the first socialist president.

**1973**
Augusto Pinochet stages a military coup and installs himself as dictator.

**1980**
A new constitution calls for a referendum in 1988.

**1988**
Voters reject a continuation of Pinochet's regime.

**1541**

Pedro de Valdivia founds Santiago.

**1553–1557**

Lautaro leads Mapuche uprising.

**1557–1810**

The Spanish vice royalty in Peru governs Chile.

**1810**

Chile declares independence from Spain.

**1813–1814**

Spain launches a successful reconquest of Chile.

**1891**

Civil war breaks out; A new constitution establishes a parliamentary republic.

**1907**

Massacre of mine workers at Iquique by the military.

**1925**

A new constitution is enacted.

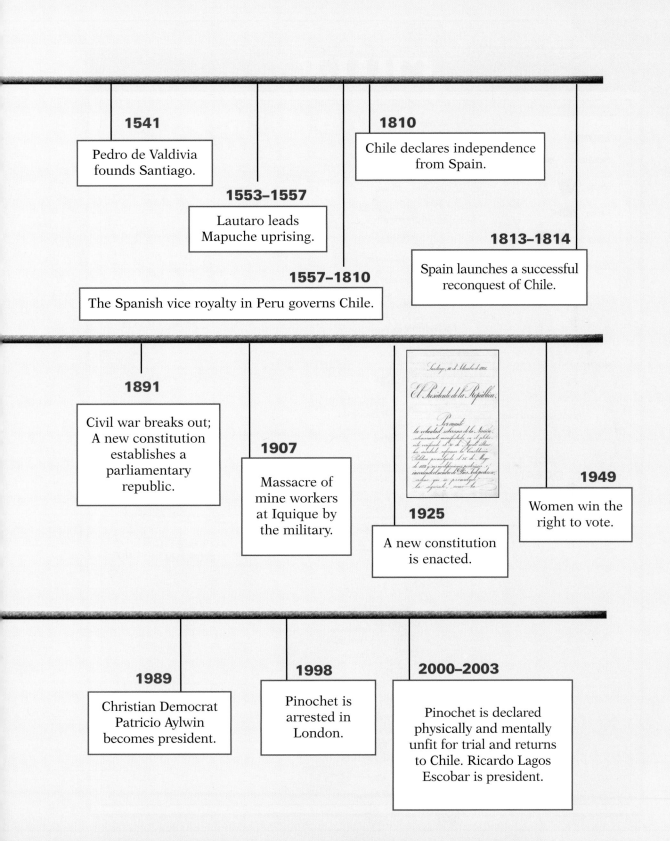

**1949**

Women win the right to vote.

**1989**

Christian Democrat Patricio Aylwin becomes president.

**1998**

Pinochet is arrested in London.

**2000–2003**

Pinochet is declared physically and mentally unfit for trial and returns to Chile. Ricardo Lagos Escobar is president.

# CHILE

**Legend**

Ports/Harbors

Mining

Fishing

Livestock

Forestry

PERU

Arica
Putre
Coscaya
**Iquique**
Pica
BOLIVIA
Caleta Lobos
Tocopilla
Calama
Toconao
**Antofagasta**
O'Higgins
PARAGUAY
Santa Catalina
Paposo
El Salvador
**Copiapó**
San Antonio
Vallenar
Sarco
BRAZIL
**La Serena**
Rivadavia
Coquimbo
Ovalle
URUGUAY
Canela Alta
Easter Island
ARGENTINA
Viña del Mar
**Valparaíso**
★ **SANTIAGO**
Navidad
• **Rancagua**
Robinson Crusoe Island
Curicó
• **Talca**
Cauquenes
Chillán
**PACIFIC OCEAN**
**Concepción**
Antuco
Recinto
Los Ángeles
Queuco
**Temuco**
Pucón
Riñihue
**Valdivia**
Lago Ranco
Osorno
Puyehue
**Puerto Montt**
Cochamó
Chacao
**ATLANTIC OCEAN**
*Chiloé Island*
Chaitén
Quellón

Puerto Cisnes
**Coihaique**
Balmaceda
Chile Chico
Cochrane
Puerto San Carlos

*FALKLAND ISLANDS (UK)*

Puerto Natales
Punta Delgada
Sombrero
**Punta Arenas**
Porvenir
Camerón

*Strait of Magellan*

# ECONOMIC FACT SHEET

**GDP in US$:** $73.4 billion

**GDP Sectors:** agriculture 8%, industry 38%, services 54% (2000)

**Land Use:** arable land 7%, meadow and pastures 16%, forests and woodland 21%, other 56%

**Currency:** U.S. equivalent: Chilean peso (CLP) Notes: 500, 1,000, 2,000, 5,000, 10,000. Coins: 1, 5, 10, 50, 100. $1 = Ch$691 (July 2002)

**Workforce:** 5.9 million. Services and government 36%; industry and commerce 34%; agriculture, forestry, and fishing 14%; construction 7%; mining 2%

**Major Agricultural Products:** wheat, corn, grapes, beans, sugar beets, potatoes, fruit, beef, poultry, wool, fish, timber

**Major Exports:** copper, fishmeal, fruits, wood products, paper products, fish, wine

**Major Imports:** petroleum, chemical products, capital goods, vehicles, electronic equipment, consumer durables, machinery

**Significant Trading Partners**: United States, European Union, Japan, Argentina, Brazil, Mexico

**Rate of Unemployment:** 8% to 10%

**Highways:** 49,585 miles (79,800 km)

**Railroads:** 4,164 miles (6,701 km)

**Waterways**: 450 miles (725 km)

**Airports:** Comodoro Arturo Benítez, commonly called Pudahuel after the neighborhood in Santiago, plus many regional airports

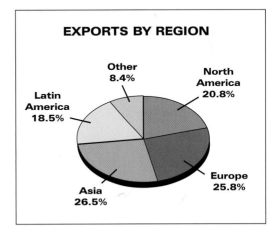

**EXPORTS BY REGION**

- Other 8.4%
- North America 20.8%
- Latin America 18.5%
- Europe 25.8%
- Asia 26.5%

# POLITICAL FACT SHEET

**Official Country Name:**
República de Chile (Republic of Chile)

**System of Government:**
Multiparty republic

**Federal Structure:** A president with executive power acts as chief of state.

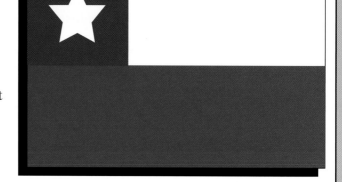

A bicameral Congress (Congreso Nacional) holds legislative power, divided between the Senate (Senado) and the Chamber of Deputies (Cámara de Diputados).

The judicial system includes the Supreme Court (Corte Suprema), appellate courts, and military courts.

**Number of Registered Voters:** 8,075,446 (2001)

**Official Flag:** Adopted in 1818. Upper half is white, representing snow on the Andes. A white star in a blue square in the upper left corner represents the powers of the state and its responsibility to the people. Blue represents the clear Chilean sky. The bottom rectangle is red for blood shed in battle.

**National Anthem:** "Himno Nacional de Chile," adopted 1941.
First composed in 1819, the lyrics of Chile's national anthem were changed in 1909 to soften the anti-Spanish message.

*Chile, your sky is a pure blue,*
*Pure breezes blow across you,*
*And your field, embroidered with*
*    flowers,*
*Is a happy copy of Eden.*
*Majestic is the snow-covered*
*    mountain*
*That was given to you by the Lord*
*    as a bastion,*

*And the sea that tranquilly washes*
*    your shore*
*Promises future splendor for you.*

*Gentle homeland, accept the vows*
*Given, Chile, on your altars,*
*That you be either the tomb of*
*    the free*
*Or a refuge from oppression.*

# CULTURAL FACT SHEET

**Official Languages:** Spanish

**Major Religions:** Roman Catholic 77%, Protestant 12%

**Capital:** Santiago

**Population:** 15.3 million

**Ethnic Groups:** Spanish-indigenous (mestizo), European, indigenous

**Life Expectancy:** Male: 72.63 years; females: 79.42 years

**Time:** Greenwich Mean Time minus four hours (GMT - 0400). Summer Daylight Savings: GMT - 0300; Easter Island is two hours behind the mainland.

**Literacy Rate:** 95.2 percent

**National Flower:** copihue

**National Bird:** Andean condor

**National Animal:** huemul

**National Tree**: *Araucaria araucana* (monkey puzzle tree)

**Cultural Leaders:**
   **Visual Arts:** Roberto Matta, Alejandro Jodorowsky, Alicia Villa Arreal
   **Literature:** Pablo Neruda, Gabriela Mistral, Isabel Allende, Antonio Skármeta
   **Music:** Victor Jara, Violeta Parra, Claudio Arrau , Inti-Illimani, Quilapayun
   **Entertainment:** Miguel Littin, Gustavo Graef-Marino, La Tropa
   **Sports:** Marlene Ahrens, world-class javelin thrower; Marcelo Ríos, tennis player
   **Soccer Teams:** Colo Colo, Universidad de Chile, Universidad Católica

## National Holidays and Festivals

January 1: **Año Nuevo** (New Year's Day)
April: **Semana Santa** (Easter Week—Good Friday and Easter Sunday are national holidays)
May 1: **Día del Trabajo** (Labor Day)
May 21: **Glorias Navales** (Navy Day)
May 30: **Corpus Christi**
June 29: **Dia de San Pedro y San Pablo** (St. Peter and St. Paul's Day)
August 15: **Asunción de la Virgen** (Assumption)

September 18: **Día de la Independencia Nacional** (Independence Day)
September 19: **Día del Ejército** (Armed Forces Day)
October 12: **Día de la Raza** (Columbus Day)
November 1: **Todo los Santos** (All Saints' Day)
December 8: **Immaculada Concepción** (Immaculate Conception)
December 25: **Navidad** (Christmas)

**Working Life:** At least 15 vacation days, in addition to public holidays. The work week of approximately 45 to 50 hours is typically from Monday through Friday.

# GLOSSARY

**animism (AN-ih-mism)** Practice of attributing conscious life to objects and natural phenomena, as in some religions.

**annulment (uh-NULL-ment)** Declared invalid or void.

**archipelago (ar-kih-PEH-lah-goe)** A chain of islands.

**avant-garde (AH-vant GARD)** A new and groundbreaking artistic movement or concept.

**Basque (BAHSK)** Peoples originally from the Pyrenees and Bay of Biscay regions of France and Spain.

**biomes (BI-ohms)** Areas characterized by the climate and life forms that live there.

**coalition (koe-uh-LIH-shun)** A temporary alliance of distinct parties, persons, or states.

**compulsory (kome-PUHL-so-ree)** Mandatory or required.

**coniferous/deciduous (kah-NIH-fur-uhs/(deh-SIHJ-oo-us)** Coniferous trees and shrubs have needlelike leaves and grow cones. The leaves of deciduous trees and plants fall off in autumn.

**conquistador (kon-KEES-tuh-dor)** A Spanish explorer who tried to take over Mexico by force in the 1500s.

**cordillera (core-dih-YEH-rah)** A chain of mountain ranges.

**epicenter (EH-pih-sen-ter)** The part of Earth's surface directly above the center of an earthquake.

**exile (EG-zyl)** To make a person leave his or her home or country.

**expatriate (ex-PAY-tree-et)** One who has left one's country of birth to live somewhere else.

**geoglyph (JEE-oh-gliff)** Ancient image created on the ground.

**hierarchy (HI-ur-ar-kee)** The classification of people according to ability, economic, social, or professional standing.

**homogenous (hohm-oh-JEE-nee-us)** Of uniform structure or composition throughout.

**indigenous (in-DIJ-in-us)** Originating, living, or occurring naturally in a particular region or environment.

**influx (IN-flucks)** Coming in or arriving in large numbers.

**junta (HUHN-tah)** A group of people controlling a government.

**Lent (LENT)** The forty weekdays before Easter when some Christians try to give up something they enjoy.

**marsupial (mar-SOO-pee-ul)** A type of animal that carries its young in a pouch.

**matriculation (mah-trick-you-LAY-shun)** Enrollment.

**montage (mon-TAZH)** A photograph or other visual artwork created from a variety of images.

**nomadic (noh-MA-dik)** Roaming about from place to place.

**regime (reh-JEEM)** A period of rule.

**repertoire (REH-per-twar)** A list of musical works that one is able to perform.

**seismic (SYZ-mick)** Earthshaking; pertaining to an earthquake or earth vibration.

**shaman (SHA-min)** A priest in some religions who uses magic to heal the sick and control or predict events in people's lives.

**subsidize (SUB-sid-eyes)** To aid or promote with public money.

**subversive (sub-VER-siv)** That which undermines or corrupts widely held beliefs or systems.

**tectonic plates (tek-TAH-nik PLAYTS)** Large segments of Earth's crust that are prone to movement.

**tribute (TRIB-yoot)** A gift or message of thanks or respect; an act of generosity toward a person.

# FOR MORE INFORMATION

Chile, a Land of Surprises
556 Yonkers Avenue
Yonkers, NY 10704
(914) 965-9127
Web site: http://www.visionchile.com

Chile Consular Information Sheet
U.S. Department of State
2201 C Street NW
Washington, DC 20520
(202) 647-4000
Web site: http://travel.state.gov/chile.html

Consulate Generals of Chile
Chicago:
John Hancock Center

875 North Michigan Avenue, Suite 3352
Chicago, IL 60611
(312) 654-8780
Web site: http://www.consuladoschile.org

Houston:
1360 Post Oak Boulevard, Suite 1330
Houston, TX 77056
(713) 963-9066
e-mail: conchihous@aol.com

Los Angeles:
1900 Avenue of the Stars, Suite 2450
Century City, CA 90067
(310) 785-0047
e-mail: cgchilela@aol.com

Miami:
800 Brickell Avenue, Suite 1230
Miami, FL, 33131
(305) 373-8623 or 373-8624
e-mail: cgmiamius@msn.com

San Francisco:
870 Market Street, Suite 1058
San Francisco, CA 94102
(415) 982-7662
e-mail: cgsfchile@aol.com

Toronto, Canada:
2 Bloor Street W, Suite 1801
Toronto, ON M4W 3E2
(416) 924-0106
e-mail: consulate@congechiletoronto.com
Web site:
    http://www.congechiletoronto.com/

Embassy of Chile
1732 Massachusetts Avenue NW
Washington, DC 20036
(202) 785-1746
e-mail: embassy@embassyofchile.org
Web site: http://www.chile-usa.org/
    ambassador.htm

## Web Sites

Due to the changing nature of Internet links, the Rosen Publishing Group, Inc., has developed an online list of Web sites related to the subject of this book. This site is updated regularly. Please use this link to access the list:

http://www.rosenlinks.com/pswc/chil/

# FOR FURTHER READING

Arnold, Caroline. *Easter Island*. New York: Houghton Mifflin Company, 2000.

Bierhorst, John. *The Mythology of South America*. New York: William Morrow and Company, 1988.

Chapman, Victoria L., and David Lindroth. *Latin American History on File*. New York: Facts on File, 1996.

Goodnough, David. *Pablo Neruda: Nobel Prize-Winning Poet*. Springfield, NJ: Enslow Publishers, 1998.

Hyndley, Kate. *The Voyage of the* Beagle. New York: Bookwright Press, 1989.

# BIBLIOGRAPHY

Bercht, Fatima. *Contemporary Art from Chile*. New York: Americas Society, 1991.

Bernhardson, Wayne. *Chile and Easter Island*. Victoria, Australia: Lonely Planet Publications, 2000.

Bureau of Western Hemisphere Affairs. "Background Note: Chile." 2002. Retrieved June 30, 2002 (http://www.state. gov/r/pa/ei/bgn/1981.htm).

Caistor, Nick. *Chile in Focus: A Guide to the People, Politics and Culture*. New York: Interlink Publishing Group, Inc., 1998.

Castillo-Feliú, Guillermo I. *Culture and Customs of Chile*. Westport, CT: Greenwood Press, 2000.

CIA Factbook 2001 (http://www.odci.gov/cia).

*Countries of the World and Their Leaders, Yearbook 2002*, Vol. 1. Farmington Hills, MI: Gale Group, 2001, pp. 407–412.

Embassy of Chile. "Cultural Affairs." 2002. Retrieved June 30, 2002 (http://www. chile-usa.org/cultural.htm).

Ethnologue. "Ethnologue Country Index." 2002. Retrieved June 30, 2002 (http://www.ethnologue.com/ country_index.asp).

*Europa World Year Book 2001*, Vol. 1. London, UK: Europa Publications, pp. 1002–1015.

Fleet, Michael, and Brian H. Smith. *The Catholic Church and Democracy in Chile and Peru*. Notre Dame, IN: University of Notre Dame Press, 1997.

Hickman, John. *News from the End of the Earth*. New York: St. Martin's Press, 1998.

Hudson, Rex A. "Chile: A Country Study." 1994. Retrieved June 30, 2002 (http://lcweb2.loc.gov/frd/cs/cltoc.html).

Minnis, Natalie, ed. *Insight Guide Chile*. Maspeth, NY: Langenscheidt Publishers, 1999.

Pino-Saavedra, Yolando. *Folktales of Chile*. Chicago: University of Chicago Press, 1967.

Roraff, Susan, and Laura Camacho. *Culture Shock Chile*. Portland, OR: Times Editions, 1999.

Toloza, Cristián, and Eugenio Lahera, eds. *Chile in the Nineties*. Stanford, CA: Stanford University Libraries, 2000.

Van Waerebeek-Gonzalez, Ruth. *The Chilean Kitchen*. New York: Penguin Putnam, Inc., 1999.

Wheeler, Sara. *Travels in a Thin Country*. New York: Random House, 1999.

Wilcock, John. *An Occult Guide to South America*. New York: The Book Division of Laurel Tape and Film, Inc., 1976.

U.S. State Department Web site. "Chile." Retrieved June 15, 2002 (http://www.state.gov/r/pa/ei/bgn/ 1981.htm).

# PRIMARY SOURCE IMAGE LIST

**Page 20:** This document established Santiago as a Spanish settlement and capital of Chile. It was signed by Pedro de Valdivia on February 2, 1541.

**Page 21:** The 1,200-year-old skeleton dubbed "Miss Chile" was discovered in the Atacama Desert. It is housed in San Pedro de Atacama.

**Page 22:** This ceremonial headdress dates from AD 300.

**Page 23:** An engraved portrait of Francisco Pizarro circa 1500.

**Page 25:** A map from 1600 showing the Straits of Magellan.

**Page 26:** *Renuncia de Bernardo O'Higgins, 1823* (Renunciation of Bernardo O'Higgins, 1823) dated 1860.

**Page 28:** The constitution of Chile from 1833.

**Page 29:** Suicide letter written on September 18, 1891, by José Manuel Balmaceda to Claudio Vicuña and Julio Bañados.

**Page 30:** Photograph of Augusto Pinochet taken around 1977.

**Page 31:** Demonstration during May Day celebration of 1978.

**Page 32:** Page one of of Chile's 1925 constitution.

**Page 33:** The last page of Chile's 1925 constitution signed by President Arturo Alessandri Palma and his cabinet members.

**Page 34:** A historic photograph of Yamana Indians, which is housed at the Museum at Puenta Arenas, southern Patagonia, Chile.

**Page 36:** A Rongorongo tablet that was discovered in 1868 on Easter Island.

**Page 44:** Petroglyphs in rocks along the slopes of the Rano Raku volcano on Easter Island.

**Page 45:** Mapuche face mask housed at the Araucania Museum in Temuco, Chile.

**Page 47:** Image of Captain Cook visiting Easter Island circa 1774, engraved in Italy.

**Page 48:** Birdman carving discovered on Easter Island.

**Page 50:** *Ngenenchen* painted by Rocio Reyes-Cortez in 1992.

**Page 61:** Church designed by Gustave Eiffel 1889 located in Herradura, Chile.

**Page 63:** *Virgin of the Merced*, a painting housed in the Museo de la Merced, Santiago, Chile.

**Page 68:** Mapuche weaving located in the Museum of Pre-Columbian Art in Santiago, Chile.

**Page 69:** Diaguita clay jar located at the Museum of Pre-Columbian Art.

**Page 70:** *Casa de la cordillera en Chillan* painted in watercolor by Luis Guzman Molina in 1997.

**Page 71:** *L'Etang de No. 1958* created by Roberto Echaurren-Matta in 1958. It is housed at the Musée National d'Art Moderne, Centre Georges Pompidou, Paris, France.

**Page 80:** Manuscript of *Canto primero de la Araucana* written by Alonso de Ercilla y Zúñiga in 1574.

**Page 81:** Photograph of Gabriela Mistral taken at the 1945 Nobel Prize ceremony in Stockholm, Sweden.

**Page 82:** Poem "Balada" handwritten by Gabriela Mistral.

**Page 82:** Photograph of Pablo Neruda taken in 1971 at the Nobel Prize ceremony in Stockholm, Sweden.

**Page 84:** Photograph of Isabel Allende dated November 3, 1998.

**Page 85:** Poem "La Capilla Aldeana" handwritten by Vincente Huidobro. It is located at the Museo Nacional Centro de Arte Reina Sofia in Barcelona, Spain.

**Page 86:** Photograph of Chilean dancers taken circa 1955.

**Page 87:** Photograph of José Donoso dated 1957.

**Page 88:** Photograph of Violeta Parra.

**Page 89:** Photograph of Claudio Arrau playing the piano taken by Lucien Aigner circa 1940.

**Page 98:** "Preparing to Smite the Ball," a copper cut appearing in Amedee Francois Frezier's *A Voyage to the South Seas Between 1712–1714*. It was printed in 1717 in London, England.

# INDEX

**About the Author**

Corona Brezina and Jason Porterfield are writers living in Chicago. They are both graduates of Oberlin College.

**Designer:** Geri Fletcher; **Cover Designer:** Tahara Hasan; **Editor:** Jill Jarnow;
**Photo Researcher:** Gillian Harper; **Photo Research Assistant:** Fernanda Rocha